SET THE COURSE

Best HR Practices for Long-Term Care Leaders

LORI L. DIEROLF

Set the Course: Best HR Practices for Long-Term Care Leaders

Lori L. Dierolf

Print ISBN: 978-1-48359-227-5

eBook ISBN: 978-1-48359-228-2

PREFACE

Growing up in the coal region of Central Pennsylvania was a unique experience, though, as with most things in life, I didn't realize it at the time. The area where I lived (neighborhood is much too fancy to apply) was outside of a very small city, and most of my neighbors were Ukrainian, like my family. It all seemed very normal to me that we would live in a house next to my grandmother; I knew plenty of people who lived just a few houses away from members of their families. As an adult, I now realize how rare and special that experience was.

It was a blessing to grow up with Nana-Next-Door (so called to differentiate between her and my other grandmother, Nana-Down-Town). When my brother, sisters, and I were young, she would take us for long walks in the woods behind our homes to pick berries or mushrooms from which she would always cook something delicious for us. Over time and as I grew older, my relationship with my grandmother grew stronger.

When I was in high school, I spent most evenings sitting with my Nana on her back porch swing, watching out for shooting stars. On those nights, we would talk about her life growing up (her mother had died when she was fourteen, so she quit school in order to raise her four siblings under a very abusive father), working in sewing factories, losing her husband to a heart attack when he was only thirty-nine, and raising three young sons on her own. She would listen to me complain about my teenage woes, which paled in comparison to her struggles, but she always was my shoulder to cry on, no matter how silly my problems might have seemed to her.

It was during these years that I began calling my grandmother by her first name, Mary, or Mare, as I fondly used to call her. My parents chastised me, saying I was disrespectful. But the truth of the matter was, Mare was so much more than a grandmother—she was my confidante, my gin rummy partner, my halupki coach, my Polish teacher (mostly curse words!), my storyteller, my biggest cheerleader, and my very best friend.

After I left for college, and later got married and had children, our Sunday night phone calls still kept us connected. Though we were separated by both age and distance at that time, we continued to enjoy an exceptional friendship, and while she passed away in 2004, not a day goes by that I don't think about her and the many ways she has colored my life.

I am certain that my relationship with my grandmother is what led me to a career in the long-term care industry. Because of Mare and the way I grew up, it never occurred to me that people might think working with the elderly to be boring or depressing. Surprisingly, though, that is the opinion of many. When I interview staff for jobs in long-term care, I often hear about how nurses want to work in a hospital, or with babies, or in rehabilitation, or in an emergency room. It is very unusual to hear from someone who enters the nursing field to want to work with the elderly in a long-term care setting.

Working with long-term residents has been a very gratifying experience for me. Unlike hospitals, staff here are able to get to know the residents well, over weeks, months, and, many times, years. Spending this amount of time with another person allows you to form a deep, personal connection. This connection is also extended to the residents' families, who are so grateful not just for the care but also for the caring provided to their loved ones. Who among us would not be put at ease knowing that if we ourselves are not able to provide all the hands-on care needs of our parents, those who are giving the care know our loved ones inside and out? And wouldn't it make you feel better if you also knew those caregivers on a personal level? Long-term care employees become part of the residents' families, and vice versa. It is an intensely satisfying part of the job.

Dianne Moody, a dietary director, puts it like this,

"It's all about the little things for me[—s]haring a laugh, a smile, a tear. It's connecting on a personal level and knowing that what you do makes a difference in their lives. Knowing they appreciate it is just icing on the cake."

Unlike employees in doctors' offices who may see the same patient for years, long-term care employees see the individual at his best, his worst, and at every stage in between. If you have ever accompanied an elderly, loved one to the doctor, you might not be surprised when all of her aches and pains mysteriously disappear on the morning of the appointment. According to her report to the doctor, she's now sleeping fine, has no problems eating, her bowels are working okay, and, of course, the arthritis doesn't bother her that much. While not every elderly patient tries to portray a picture of perfect health (some go in the opposite direction!), my point is that seeing someone for a few minutes every month does not allow for a true, overall picture of how the individual is really doing or what the state of her health really is.

Helping residents in a long-term care setting also allows staff to feel the heartfelt appreciation of these special people. Often, the smallest things can mean the world to them. For some, the five minutes you spend talking about your plans for the weekend or your son's soccer game are the highlight of their day! During one of our regular meetings, my friend Howard shared with me that none of his friends in the facility knew any good jokes. As a result, every few weeks I would type up a few pages of jokes from the internet and tape them to his door while he was out of his room. I know he carries them around in his walker to share with his visitors and friends. While it takes only a few minutes of my time, I know he's secretly waiting for the next one to appear, and when he sees that envelope on his door, he smiles!

I would be remiss if I did not address the fact that losing residents to death is also a very real part of working in long-term health care. Learning to deal with the passing of a resident is a necessary part of the job but is one for which all long-term care employees must prepare for. As you can imagine, this is not easy to do, especially when an extraordinary bond exists between an employee and the resident. But this is the nature of working in the long-term care environment.

Erika Miranda, an RN, describes it this way,

"With each resident that has passed away under my care, knowing I did my very best in caring for them while they were living, I felt like I needed to see it through and be there for them when they passed away. It's like continuing my promise to them by taking care of them until the end. I cope by reminding myself that I kept my promise."

Most employees feel, as I do, that being with someone, helping him or her to pass on, is an intensely intimate experience that few people have the honor of experiencing in their work. For those in long-term care, knowing that they have provided another human being with dignity and comfort at the end of their life's journey is a gift to be cherished, not a burden to be avoided. And while losing residents takes an emotional toll, it is worth the price to have been there when they needed us the most, when they needed us the last.

LPN Ingrid Shaeffer says,

"I actually don't cope well with residents dying, especially my favorites. I cry every Time[—]I'm human, and I tend to wear my heart on my sleeve. But I stay because there's always another person to help."

With a better understanding of the humans who make up your human resources (HR) in long-term care, it is my intent that this book provides you with useful information, real-life examples, and helpful suggestions for building up your employees, valuing what they bring to your organization, and providing them with the structure, consistency, and respect that will make them and you successful.

CHAPTER ONE

WHY WRITE THIS BOOK

"Character cannot be developed in ease and quiet. Only through experience of trial and suffering can the soul be strengthened, ambition inspired, and success achieved."

Helen Keller

In 1991, I graduated from Millersville University of Pennsylvania with a Bachelor's degree in psychology and had absolutely no idea what I wanted to do with the rest of my life. I followed some of my friends to graduate school to study clinical psychology, and at first, I thought it would be a good career for me. After all, I really did enjoy helping people and solving problems.

In my second year of graduate school, I took a class where I was required to videotape myself counseling a student volunteer. I had to submit to my professor my assessment information, progress, and updates on how the sessions were going. My professor reviewed the tapes, oversaw the counseling process, and provided input on my counseling abilities during the sessions. As problems go, my students were very vanilla—not getting along with mother, mainly because mother didn't like boyfriend—not a bad case to start with, I thought.

I took my counseling responsibilities very seriously and went to great lengths in my efforts to help this young lady. I researched information on mother–daughter relationships to share with her. I investigated how I could best communicate with a young adult so that she would be receptive to thoughts and ideas. I developed suggestion after suggestion to help improve the problems she identified in her life. And after ten weeks of counseling, she had not changed one single thing. Worse than that, when I pointed out to her that despite our hours of meeting, nothing had changed. . .she simply smiled and shrugged her shoulders!

It was then that I realized that counseling was not the profession for me. I am a person who thrives on making a difference, on solving problems, on conquering life's challenges one at a time. For my own sanity, I had to accept the fact that I cannot change people who do not want to change themselves. It was at this time that I also developed a phrase I still use today to help people who seem to be unable to get out of their own way: When you have a problem, you always have two choices. You can choose to do something, or you can choose to do nothing, but if you choose to do nothing, you have also lost the right to complain about it anymore.

And so, to the disappointment of my parents ("How are you going to support yourself?") as well as my graduate school friends (They said, "you only have a year left—just finish!"), I quit my graduate school program and began looking for a job. There are not many options for someone with a BA in psychology—or at least there were not many in 1993. I began working in personal care group homes for individuals who were developmentally challenged. The work included personal care and hygiene tasks that no one ever really showed me how to do. What I did learn, which was paramount, though, was that these clients were not just their diseases—they were people, real human beings with feelings and dreams and jobs and families who loved them. Working with them and getting to know them warmed my heart, and I loved them.

As this work did not pay very well and my student loans were looming large, I took a second job in a rehabilitation program for individuals with traumatic brain injuries. I spent time working in their personal care program as well as in their day clinic, helping clients with various physical and cognitive exercises. Over time, however, I was asked to assume more responsibility in the personal care facility, and eventually I began working there full time as a supervisor. My duties included assisting with training new staff, creating schedules and work checklists, assisting with interviewing and hiring paperwork, and ensuring compliance with the company's accreditation organization—all of which I enjoyed.

One day while reading the newspaper, I saw a classified ad for a "Human Resources Director," which indicated the job responsibilities would be hiring and training employees, maintaining compliance with state agencies, and providing leadership. I thought, "I do that!" I did not know what "Human Resources" meant before that day, but it sounded perfect for me. I applied, interviewed, and despite having no true HR experience, was hired at a skilled nursing facility. Since that time, I have worked in other skilled facilities, as well as in a continuing care retirement community (with independent living, personal care, skilled nursing care, and dementia care) and in a personal care community. And while all of these positions are considered long-term care, they each had their own specific HR challenges.

In addition to working in these various types of long-term care facilities, I have also worked for a large corporation with more than two hundred facilities across the country; a small corporation with eight local facilities; a large not-for-profit organization with more than two thousand residents; and a small, family-owned, for-profit company with less than one hundred seventy-five residents in two locations. All of this to say, when it comes to HR in long-term care, I have seen and learned a lot over the past twenty years. If my successes and failures can make one leader's day in a long-term care facility easier, I would have achieved my goal.

As had happened to me, many employees in health care settings who show dedication and initiative tend to be recognized and *rewarded* with more responsibility. I point this out because, despite the fact that in many industries, those who work as HR professionals tend to have degrees in HR or business, individuals who work as HR professionals in health care may or may not have a degree at all, let alone one in HR. I have met a number of HR professionals who were RNs or LPNs, as well as others, who simply worked in the business department for so many years that they eventually just took over the HR function when it became available because they were good at paperwork and were reliable.

The reality for many long-term care facilities is that while the person doing the HR function may understand his or her day-to-day duties, he or she may not necessarily have the soft skills such as tactfulness or the ability to be an active listener that are so essential to being the customer service representative for employees. Also, this means that other supervisors in the facility either do not receive any guidance in proper HR practices or that training is left to the facility's administrator. . .and, let's be honest, in the heat of the battle in long-term care, this type of training is very low on the list of priorities for that busy individual. As the saying goes, "you can't give what you don't have." And you cannot teach what you yourself do not know.

What kinds of HR practices am I talking about? I mean things such as keeping your company from being sued and making your employees love working with you. In the first case, I refer to such things as not asking someone's age during an interview or not reducing someone's hours because she used her approved intermittent Family Medical Leave (FMLA). If someone had not explicitly educated you about these things, how would you have learned them, as such things cannot be considered common knowledge?

In the second instance, many leaders are task-focused and believe that they are doing a great job when all the work is getting done. Unfortunately, if you are not also monitoring the pulse of your employees' morale, you are really only doing half the job. I have worked with supervisors who hang their hats on perfect state surveys but fail to see how miserable and unmotivated their employees are or the fact that they play a role in impacting the morale of those employees. I believe that it is an HR professional's role to ensure he or she, as well as the facility's supervisors, always monitor employee satisfaction in the organization. All the paperwork may get done, but a facility where employees are unhappy is a facility where resident care suffers. Leadership guru Dr. John Maxwell says, "Managers work with processes[—]leaders work with people." HR professionals should strive to be leaders, not managers.

This leads to the third and the most important reason I write this book: employee turnover. *The Journal of Applied Gerontology* published an article in May 2009 that stated that the national turnover for LPNs in long-term care was 51 percent; for RNs, 56.1 percent; and for CNAs, a whopping 64.5 percent! Having lived in Lancaster County, Pennsylvania, throughout my HR career, I know firsthand the challenges of staff retention. This marketplace is saturated with retirement communities, and employees can easily quit one facility in the morning and have a job offer in another facility by the afternoon.

Employee turnover has a huge impact on any company, but this is especially true in a long-term care facility where you are working against the clock. It has been my experience that for every six applications I receive, only one is qualified for the position for which I am interviewing (we will discuss this more in chapter 4). It has also been my experience that for every four people I interview, only one will actually become an employee. This, coupled with the number of pre-employment requirements by licensing agencies or company health and safety policies (criminal background checks, FBI clearances, physicals, two-step tuberculosis (TB) tests, drug screens, etc.), means that even after I have found the perfect candidate for the position, it will still take almost two weeks to get the person onto the floor to begin training. When a candidate really needs a job, that's a long time to wait, especially when they could be working the next day at the mall!

For long-term care employees, there is another significant difference between working in health care and working in retail—commitment. For example, if Jennifer does not come to work at the department store, her register is closed and customers have to go to another register and maybe wait in a longer line. Health-care facilities do not work this way. Facilities must calculate the number of hours that employees are providing care each day and may never provide fewer than the state-regulated number of care hours per day according to the regulations of their licensing agency. That means if Jennifer is a CNA, and she doesn't show for her shift, *someone* will be required to cover that shift. It also means scrambling to find last-minute coverage, making frantic phone calls, and begging employees who have already worked a full shift to stay a little longer and, in most situations, paying someone overtime.

I have noticed a very strange phenomenon about overtime, and this has remained constant no matter what type of long-term care facility I am working at. Almost every person I interview wants as much overtime as he or she can get. They are eager, excited at the thought of earning extra money, but after their first sixty days as an employee, almost none of those people feel the same way. I am sure you can guess what happens to them—they become burned out.

This problem is systemic. At any given time, an average-size long-term care facility has some open positions in its nursing department. That means, when the schedule is created, those openings need to be filled. The scheduler talks with employees who agree to work the shifts for which there are openings, in addition to their normally scheduled hours. If the resident care hours per day are acceptable to them, it may also mean shifting employee work assignments around. By this I mean that the total number of care hours are on target, so instead of getting another person to come in, one person may be assigned three wings instead of two, or someone may be reassigned to a different unit completely for the entire shift. In the best case scenario, someone may offer to work a double shift or another employee may come in early and have a supervisor work the first half of the shift on the floor. Add a call off, and the whole plan is blown to bits.

Employee turnover also impacts an organization's budget, and not just because of overtime. The cost of bringing new employees into a long-term care facility is significant. This includes the hours and hours that the HR professional takes to recruit, interview, hire, and orient candidates; the cost for all the pre-employment requirements; as well as paid time to the new employee for his or her orientation and on-the-floor training (during which they are still not technically completing a full workload because they are still learning the job). Now imagine, as the previous statistic showed, that two out of every three individuals that you hired left within the first six months.

Employee morale is always impacted by high turnover, though it is not something that we can measure as easily as the finances. Those who work in health care usually have gotten into that field because they have huge hearts for helping people. They hate to see others in pain or in need, so they do whatever they can whenever they can to make sure everyone is taken care of. Unfortunately, it also means they get asked to help too often, and if other employees rely on that one person to pick up shifts all the time, that may also lead to resentment, or burn-out, or both.

This, in turn, can lead to employees simply being too exhausted to carry out their work duties to their fullest potential. Imagine lifting a two-hundred-pound resident onto and off a toilet or into and out of a bed or wheelchair repeatedly for sixteen hours. Things get missed, which leads to care being good enough, but not great. Quality is sacrificed, and your residents and their families notice. Working at the mall is starting to sound better and better, isn't it?

Finally, no matter how great she was at running the register or at helping a customer find the right dress, when Jennifer leaves that department store job to move to another state, it is not likely that her customers are going to miss her, or cry for her, or stop eating when she is gone, or refuse to bathe ever again. Working in long-term care means becoming a member of the residents' families. They experience a loss when someone important to them leaves employment. It is not the same as working in a doctor's office, or a hospital, or a clinic. The relationships are simply not comparable to spending time with caregivers for eight or twelve or sixteen hours a day for weeks and months and years.

That's why this book is written specifically for individuals in long-term care. They are a special group of people with very intricate HR issues, and they deserve a little help along the way.

CHAPTER TWO

FOR WHOM IS THIS BOOK INTENDED?

*"I'm not telling you it's going to be easy.
I'm telling you it's going to be worth it."*

Art Williams

There are three categories of long-term care employees I have in mind as I write this book. The first, obviously, is the HR professional. Less obviously, though, there are subgroups that need to hear the information for different reasons. The second category is administrators and the third is leaders and supervisors.

HR Professionals in Long-Term Care

One thing I believe about HR professionals in long-term care is that once they are in their position, they tend to stay put. There are a number of reasons I think this is true. First, it is excruciatingly painful to learn the long-term care industry. At one point in my career, I had an administrator who told her staff there were more regulations for a nursing home in the Commonwealth of Pennsylvania than there were for a nuclear power plant (I have no way of knowing if this was true!).

If you work in a continuing care retirement community, there are more than one set of regulations to follow, though in hiring practices, it is generally decided to comply with the agency whose regulations are most stringent and apply them to all employees, no matter what level of care they will be working in. I have had my share of disagreements with supervisors in independent living who need employees and do not understand or care that their new hires must complete a two-step test for TB before they can wash dishes in their kitchen. Rules are rules.

As mentioned in the last chapter, the revolving door of employees in long-term care is too much for some HR professionals to handle. At one facility where I was hired in June, I calculated the annual turnover rate the following January to have been 217 percent! For those of you who are having trouble wrapping your brain around how turnover could be more than a hundred percent, let me explain. The number is calculated using the number of employees hired in the year and the number of employees who left in the year. If you lost almost every employee that you hired *and* you also lost people who were hired in years prior to that year, voila!, more than a hundred percent turnover!

The most difficult period of time for a new HR professional is the first twelve to twenty-four months. During this time, they are assessing the state of affairs, finding out what they don't yet know, establishing themselves with the key people in the facility, and laying the foundation on which they will build their own HR practices and protocols. After the first year, they begin to have a rhythm. And after all that work and effort has paid off and systems are in place, why would an HR professional want to leave? This is why I say that once they settle into their positions, HR professionals in long-term care tend to stay. After all, leaving a position right after all the heavy lifting has been done, for another position that will immediately also require one to two more years of heavy lifting, seems counterintuitive.

In settings such as long-term care, employee relationships are different than in other industries. Staff are more than important; they are imperative. And the most fundamental thing to expect from them is care. Working with people in a health-care setting is a very personal, intimate experience. It is watching people that we love die, sometimes slowly day-by-day, sometimes suddenly in the middle of the night. It is celebrating when someone with a broken hip finally takes that first walk down the hall without his walker. A person could not possibly deal with the emotional ups and downs of this kind of work without the strong and caring system of co-worker support that long-term care facilities have. All of this to say, once an HR professional becomes invested, it is a very difficult position to leave.

HR professionals care about their residents, as well. And while working for the same company for your entire career is said to be a thing of the past, many of the HR professionals I knew fifteen years ago still work for the same facility today, though some have advanced in their positions in that time. But even as a hard-core, seasoned HR professional in long-term care, it is always nice to find new and innovative ways to refresh our programs or update our ways.

As I have discussed why many HR professionals stay in their positions, let me now address a situation where this is generally not the case—a facility with a troubled reputation. If a long-term care facility's reputation is average or above average, retaining an HR professional may not be an issue. But in facilities where the reputation is below average or poor, it is a completely different story. This can go one of two ways.

If the company pays well and they find an energetic problem-solver who thrives on a challenge, they can hire an HR professional with the exact experience in long-term care that is needed. However, those people are sometimes hard to find (especially if they are nice and warm and cozy in the job where they just settled in after finishing all the heavy lifting!). If that person does not show up at the doorstep, the next-best candidate is the one who is unfamiliar with the industry (and, therefore, your reputation), and is looking to branch out, explore, gain new experience, or whatever other buzzwords are used when applying for a position for which a person has little comparable experience.

Whether they are new to HR in general (as I was) or new to the long-term care industry, new HR professionals with the right training and support will benefit from the information to be covered in this book, written by someone who has been in the trenches.

I would like to return briefly to the topic of facility reputation. It is amazing the difference that a facility's reputation has on the HR functions in long-term care. I have worked in my share of facilities with troubled reputations. Note here that I said the *reputation* was troubled. I have worked in more than one facility where the reputation was below average or even poor, but the care, state inspections, and staff morale were great! It is very hard to reinvent your facility once it gets that stigma. It can be done, but it takes years of excellence and intentionality of marketing to make sure the community and other facilities can see the improvements. Until that happens, recruitment will be a challenge. Employees want to be proud of the place where they work and they want to be associated with great caregiving.

So, for the long-term care HR professionals out there—the ones who have made their careers in the health-care industry and are looking to breathe some new life into what they have been doing for the last twenty years—this book is for you.

For the industry transplants—those who thought working in a beautiful office and wearing professional clothing would be a nice change of pace—buckle up! This book will help you navigate your way through those critical first twenty-four months in long-term care (hopefully without the compulsion to rip every hair out of your head).

And finally, for those new to the HR profession, this book is especially for you! Remember chapter 1 where I told you that I had no real HR experience and I was hired to work in a skilled nursing facility? Well, there's more to that story. . . .

I spent the first day and a half in my new role as the HR director being trained by the person I was replacing. She had begun her career in the manufacturing industry, and she told me she was going back "to where the money was." After those days, I was on my own. Please understand that at no point, either on my resume or during my interview, did I represent myself as having more experience in HR than I actually had. I shared my enthusiasm and gratitude for the opportunity to learn, and it was graciously given to me.

During my second week in that position, my administrator came into my office and closed the door. As she stood in front of my desk, arms crossed, she said to me, "Exactly what is it that you do here?"

Instantly my face started burning and I began to recite all the tasks that my predecessor had told me to do and reminded her that this was my first HR job. She responded, "Quite frankly, a monkey could do that! We don't have time for you to *learn* your job—we need you to *do* your job!"

Through my anger and humiliation, I tried to explain that I was doing everything I thought I was supposed to do, but if there were other things, she could simply tell me what they were and I would gladly do them. I think the truth was that she did not know what those things were. She just knew that things were not running smoothly, and there was simply no time for a kink in the chain in a long-term care facility.

My mom tells the story of when I was little and she would spank me, I would not cry. Honestly, even when I was that young, I knew she was only spanking me so I *would* cry, so why should I give her the satisfaction? Besides that, it didn't really hurt, so what was there to cry about? Let me tell you this not to encourage you to or discourage you from spanking your children but to illustrate that willful children grow into stubborn adults.

I left work that day very angry not just because I was demeaned by this woman but because she assumed that I *knew* what needed to be done yet I purposely chose not to do it. I spent five hours that evening typing every single thing that I had been trained to do, exactly how I was doing it, and adding all the questions that I had for each category, to make sure my understanding of the job was complete. This resulted in a thirteen-page document that I submitted to my administrator in person first thing the following morning. I also supplied additional copies for the regional HR manager and the director of nursing (DON) to review.

As it happened, I had not been doing what was needed to be done to be a successful HR director up to that point, but over the course of the next few weeks, I learned what I needed to learn and began getting everything done! Over the following six months I worked sixty-hour weeks, including interviewing at 9 p.m. and conducting orientation on Saturdays—whatever it took to get the job done. But I didn't just do those things, I finally understood that sense of urgency that was, and still is, so intensely a part of the HR role in long-term care.

Let me tell you, this was a hard lesson to learn, but one of my most precious memories of that first HR experience occurred on my last day in that position. My administrator pulled me aside and apologized for her harshness that day in my office. She hugged me and told me I was the best HR person she had ever had. I don't harbor any ill will toward her at all; she helped me become the HR person I am today. And though her method was rough, I understand that she was frustrated. The reason was simple: in long-term care, your HR profession will either make you or break you.

So, take heart, new HR professionals! There is much to learn, but my goal is to spare you from having to learn the hard way (and hopefully, without being compared to a monkey!).

Administrators in Long-Term Care

I once received a phone call at work from a friend and former co-worker who had been my marketing director in not one but two facilities. She had been working for another company at that time and she told me that her president had asked her, "Don't you know anybody with half a brain that I could hire and train to be an assistant administrator?" My friend said she did, and then she called me.

Still unsure if this was meant to be a compliment, I shared with her that I really was not looking to make a change. I had been in my current position for eighteen months at that time, so the heavy lifting was done and I was ready to enjoy the spoils for a few years. By the end of the call, I had agreed to a breakfast meeting. Eight months later, I was an assistant administrator for a personal care community.

At no point in my formal training (which at the time was forty hours in a classroom and eight hours with members of our state licensing agency, getting oriented to regulations) was anything about HR management introduced, explained, or even mentioned to my fellow administrator students.

I have had the great honor of working for and working with some amazing administrators in my career—professionals with the natural ability to lead a team, create a vision, add value to each team member, and encourage excellence without my ever needing someone to tell them how important their human resources are. I have also worked with some real duds—people who viewed their role with employees as secondary to literally everything else they needed to do. It is true: administrators have an awesome responsibility and an impossible workload, but it is my opinion that you can never be an exceptional administrator without understanding your HR responsibilities.

The administrator at my first HR job knew things were not going as well as they should, but despite her knowledge and experience, she did not have a full understanding of the role her HR director played. I like to think my thirteen-page dissertation helped illuminate her and that, as a result, we both grew through that experience.

So, administrators, this book is also for you—to allow you to gain a better understanding as to what to expect from your HR professionals and ways to support him or her with your facility's leaders, supervisors, and frontline staff. One final gift you may receive from this is the retention of your HR professional. As many of us know, "Employees don't leave jobs—they leave supervisors."

Take, for example, the administrator with whom I met to explain that the DON was not legally permitted to deny an employee's FMLA claim if all the eligibility requirements were met. He responded that he was "willing to take that legal risk" to keep the DON happy. I was shocked! In response, I told him that I could not work for an administrator or a company that was not willing to follow federal labor laws, to which he responded, "Look, it's a lot easier to replace an HR director than it is to replace a DON, so if you need to resign, go ahead." I did, and I did.

Often, HR professionals are the ones who need to tell leaders and supervisors (not to mention frontline staff) things they don't want to hear or things they simply do not agree with. Without the full understanding and support of their administrators, it is just not worth the fight. If you happen to be an administrator who has turned over more than a few HR professionals, it may be a good time to take a closer look at how you are supporting the individuals in this role. Are you making their jobs harder or easier?

This book is also meant to assist administrators in small long-term care facilities. In Pennsylvania alone, there are more than a thousand personal care homes, many of which have fewer than ten residents. It is unrealistic to think these facilities have the need or the finances to pay an HR professional to be on staff. So those HR duties fall squarely on the shoulders of the administrators (who, in many cases, are also wearing the hats of owners). For these busy individuals, wouldn't it be nice if someone wrote a book to make the HR part of what they did easier?

Leaders and Supervisors in Long-Term Care

In long-term care, the hierarchy of the nursing department varies slightly based on the level of care of the facility and their regulations. Skilled nursing facilities (SNFs), known to everyone else in the world as nursing homes, usually have people with RN licenses or

BSN or MSN degrees leading their nursing departments. Obviously, the more education they have, the more likely these DONs are to have gained some basic knowledge of leadership (a college in my area offers a class called Transforming Healthcare through Leadership in Nursing for its BSN students).

None of these individuals, however, study the ins and outs of the HR practices they will need to understand and utilize to be effective in their jobs. Such things include, for example, why it takes so long to hire an employee, what can disqualify a great applicant from being hired, or why you don't just fire employees that you want terminated. Not having a clear understanding in these areas can lead to unnecessary and unwarranted frustration with their HR professional, which can, in turn, lead to communication problems and lack of trust.

SNFs are required by regulation in Pennsylvania to have licensed RNs in their facilities twenty-four hours a day, but personal care homes (PCHs) are licensed by a different agency and have a completely different set of regulations. In Pennsylvania, PCHs are not required to have licensed nurses in the facility at all times, though in my experience, many larger facilities choose to hire LPNs owing to the acuity of resident needs, as well as the fact that these individuals have more education and experience than their medication technician (med tech) counterparts.

LPNs are those who have successfully passed a state board examination after completing a training course that in many cases takes less than two years. During their training, they complete clinical rotations in different health-care settings and take turns being a leader of their fellow students during that experience. How do I know this, you ask, if I have never been to a nursing school?

An interview question that I ask every LPN is Tell me about your leadership experience. If they have not held management positions in other jobs prior to nursing school (thankfully, many have), the most common response I get to that question is undoubtedly about the day or two they spent as the team leader in their clinical rotations. This experience is highlighted by "making sure everyone is okay" and "jumping in to help, if they need me." Therefore, the real-life leadership training is left to the long-term care employer of these nurses—their HR professional, their administrator, their DONs, and other nursing supervisors.

I mentioned that Pennsylvania's personal care homes are not required by regulations to have licensed nurses in the facility at all times. In Pennsylvania, regulations for PCHs do not require those who administer medications or give insulin or administer eye drops to have a nursing license. Instead, employees must complete a two-day, state-approved med tech training course, pass an observed skills test, and receive additional training in diabetes and insulin management from a certified diabetes educator (a class that usually lasts two to three hours). Am I painting a picture?

Without adequate training in leadership and basic HR practices, long-term care facilities are setting nurses and med techs up to fail. And all of this is in the nursing department alone! Leaders in the housekeeping, laundry, dietary, and activities departments are even less likely to have leadership experience. This is because, just like me when I worked in the facility with clients with traumatic brain injuries, if you do a good job and show potential, you are rewarded with more responsibility, which can include becoming the director of a department.

Very few long-term care facilities invest the time, effort, and money necessary to develop leadership and HR training programs for their supervisors. Often, this is because so much of what needs to be done on a day-to-day basis in long-term care is *reactive*—solving the problems as they arise. Leadership training is considered *proactive*—trying to solve a problem before it occurs by educating your team on preventing the problem in the first place.

I had an administrator who frequently reminded me that, for PCH nursing staff purposes, leadership training didn't count. What she was referring to was the fact that each member of the nursing department was required annually to complete twelve hours of training for direct care nursing, which included health care-related topics only (glaucoma, CPR, stroke, etc.), not leadership. This comment also illustrates a common complaint of many leaders in long-term care settings: "I barely have time for the training I'm required to do – where am I supposed to find time for *extra* training?!"

For each of you, it is my intention that by reading this book you will gain a better understanding of the HR function in your facilities and be able to work more closely with your HR professional or become a superstar HR professional yourself!

CHAPTER THREE

YOUR
EMPLOYEE RELATIONSHIPS

"Always treat your employees exactly how you want them to treat your best customers."

Steven R. Covey

There are plenty of books out there that will tell you how to have great relationships with your employees. It is likely that many of the suggestions you will see in this chapter would be useful in any industry, but in health care in general, and in long-term care specifically, relationships in the workplace take on much greater meaning than in an office or a store or a warehouse. Long-term care employees are meant to be more than just nice, kind, and helpful.

In long-term care, we share the common experience of helping a group of once vibrant, independent people to live out the last years (or weeks or days) of their lives with dignity, purpose, and normalcy in surroundings that are filled with understanding, acceptance, and love. By merely doing these jobs, we make ourselves vulnerable every day, because sooner or later, all of our residents leave us, which means we have an unknown yet limited amount of time to make sure they are safe, happy, healthy, and fulfilled.

It takes a special kind of person to work with the elderly in a long-term care environment. While some might say that people get used to death or get hardened by the passing of residents, I have never found that to be true. What I *have* found are caring professionals who return after their shift (off the clock) to sit with a resident, holding her hand while she actively dies—just so she doesn't pass alone. I have seen long-term care employees comforting families, completing the necessary calls to doctors and funeral homes, finishing the state-required paperwork, and then walking away and privately crying their hearts out over the loss of their friend.

While our environment is about adding life to the years of seniors, the inevitability of death is always present in the back of the minds of long-term care employees. Most people who enter the health-care field don't do it in the hopes of getting rich—they do it because they have the heart for making a difference for others. As in other settings where such strong emotions like grief, shock, and loss are present, people in long-term care become very close to each other very quickly; they rely on each other and share deeper feelings with more frequency and ease with each other, because not doing so weighs very heavily on a person. Not doing so can break you.

With this keen appreciation for the fragility of life, we tuck away our fear of losing our friends and do our best to seize the day every day, to add value to their lives however we can, and to focus on the living that is still left to do.

Employees who work in long-term care are not your average employees. Oh, they may start out that way, but if they stick around for any period of time, they won't remain that way. Take, for example, my seventeen-year-old son. He was hired as a dietary aide in a long-term care facility a year and a half ago; today, a part of his daily routine is to check the obituaries to see if any of his residents have passed away since he last worked. I didn't teach him that; he just cares about them.

So, as an HR professional who has had the honor of working with these amazing and wonderful long-term care employees for so many years, this chapter reviews the importance of having successful, engaging relationships with this special group of people.

Things to Keep in Mind

Respect

As a new HR professional, earning the respect of your employee customers is the number one, most critical priority on your to-do list. The good news? Once you have earned their respect, the other HR tasks become easier. The bad news? You must earn it one encounter at a time, one person at a time, and it always happens very slowly.

In my experience, I have also noticed that some communities are more willing to give you opportunities to earn trust than others. For example, in one facility, only the administrator and the marketing director spoke to me when I first began working. When I asked them what was going on, they told me that most of the staff lived in the small town where the facility was located (I did not and neither did the administrator or the marketing director), and if the staff didn't know you, they didn't trust you. . .you had to *earn* that.

I recently asked some of my former employees how a good HR professional shows his or her staff that they are respected. One respondent, Debbi, a med tech and personal care aide said,

"A good HR person is able to be connected and get close to employees without crossing boundaries, but still maintains the relationship with employees to show they are more than just a body for meeting hours' requirements."

Everyone wants to feel important. Successful HR professionals achieve this when they remember that every employee is their customer and that they must always put their customers first. Make time to speak with them when they need to talk, and give them your undivided attention. I apologized for being late to many meetings in my career because I had an employee in my office who was upset. At that moment, they were my top priority.

It is difficult to make employees feel important and to earn their respect if they never see you. Part of the challenge for any company that runs twenty-four hours a day is making sure those who work off shifts don't feel like second class citizens. For a successful HR professional, this means staying late, coming in early, having office hours on a Saturday, and being as flexible as you can to be accessible to each of your employees.

My regular routine for many years was to stay late every Monday. Once the bustle of the day shift died down (at that time, my office was in the center of the building, just off the lobby, where there was always lots of traffic!), I would open my door and do the paperwork. Second shift staff knew I was there if they needed anything. Many were grateful when I would relieve them of the angry family member, the walk-in tour, or the police officers who arrived because a resident on the secured dementia unit called 911 (again).

But there were also employees who regularly came to discuss concerns or problems on that day. This included night shift staff who counted on me still being there when they came in early to speak with me. About once a month, I would stay until 11:00 p.m. so that I could *see* third shift staff and greet them with one of my catch-phrases, "Welcome to work! Thanks for being here!"

Seeing employees is an essential concept. This does not mean *looking* at them (to catch them out of uniform or to find them wearing their facial piercings!). It means getting to know their faces and demeanors well enough to recognize when something is wrong. Another former employee Roshonda, an LPN, put it like this,

"A good HR person shows respect when she recognizes a person is overwhelmed, and steps in so they can step away."

Seeing your staff when they arrive for work gives you a great opportunity to practice names and learn faces. Small talk at that time also helps you learn a little about their life outside of work, which is important when your ultimate goal is to demonstrate to your employees that you value them. When you learn that someone's grandmother is receiving hospice services or that someone's sister is about to have a baby, it gives you a glimpse into your employees' sorrows and joys. Caring enough to ask how their loved ones are doing helps your team members believe that they are not just *a body* to fill a spot on the schedule.

Another essential guideline for long-term care HR professionals to gain the respect of their staff is to *get in there!* While I am not implying that you need to get a license or certification and start providing resident care to be successful in your position (although for those of you who *are* trained, we will talk more about you in a little while), I am saying that you have to be willing to help with the day-to-day, non-care issues that come up *as needed*.

For example, on Monday evenings, I would answer phones after the receptionist had left for the day. When I did not work in the evening, that responsibility fell on the nursing staff, so I got in there. At times, a resident would need some one-on-one attention, either because they were confused and exit-seeking or because they were upset about something that occurred that day, or any number of other reasons. Someone needed to sit with them, or take a walk with them, or just listen to them with a sympathetic ear. I got in there.

For physical plant issues like the front door not closing, or the alarms going off for no reason, or when a dog walked in through the automatic doors, I was in the building, so I got in there. All of these things would have required the nursing staff on second and third shifts to handle them, in addition to performing all of their other daily duties, which are extremely time-sensitive. For example, nurses and/or med techs only have a two-hour window in which to administer medications to their residents. After that time, it is considered *a medication error*, which then requires phone calls to family members, doctors, and licensing agencies, not to mention the paperwork involved!

If you want to convey the message to your employees that *they are just as important as you are*, then you need to ensure that your actions are consistent with that concept by showing that *their time is as valuable as your time*. This is what staff mean when they say they want leaders to *walk the talk*.

More than one former employee have mentioned that they feel respected when an HR professional, an administrator, or a supervisor asks them for their input, opinions, or suggestions when trying to solve a problem that directly impacts that employee's work. Extra points are earned when their feedback is later put into place (so if you don't plan on even considering your employees' ideas, don't bother asking them for it—it does more harm than good to the trust in that relationship).

If an employee's suggestion has been considered and found to be nonviable, it is important to report it back to that employee. I am not advocating the practice of giving employees more details than necessary from a business standpoint, as that is not always appropriate, but if the answer is *no*, staff appreciate knowing that. Likewise, if an issue is still being reviewed or considered, employees appreciate when managers let them know that, too. As one former employee said, "We want to know it's still in progress, and that it didn't get dropped."

In October 2006, after the shooting in Lancaster County's West Nickel Mines School, a housekeeper in one of my facilities asked me if our company had a policy in case such a tragedy happened here. We didn't, but we obviously needed one. Over the next few weeks, the company developed a policy, had safety professionals review it, and then introduced it to our staff, making sure that the housekeeper got credit for her suggestion and reinforcing that feedback is welcomed and appreciated.

As I mentioned previously, my office in one of my previous positions was located near the center of all of the action. Often during day shift, it was necessary to keep my door closed, not only to maintain confidentiality (residents sat right outside my door all day long) but also to block out the noise while interviewing or on the telephone or even trying to concentrate on paperwork. So, when I next introduce the importance of an *open door policy*, please note that I do not believe your door needs to be literally open all the time. Mine certainly wasn't.

A former med tech said this in response to my question about respect,

"Just listen. Let people come to your office and let their hair down and vent, without being afraid they are going to get [in] trouble for complaining."

Being an *active listener* is vital as a leader and as an HR person. This includes turning off your computer screen (or at least turning away from it) and muting your desk phone or not answering it when you are speaking with an employee. If you are truly not available when an employee comes to talk, set up an appointment to meet with them as soon as possible; or better yet, offer to go find them as soon as you become available (this is another way I try to show employees that they are just as important as I am—why should *they* always have to be the ones to leave their work area?).

I wonder if it would make my parents feel better to know how often I use what I learned in those two years of my clinical psychology graduate program. Often, the issues staff want to share with me are only peripherally about work; they usually focus on events happening in their personal lives that are impacting or will impact their schedule, their work performance, their transportation, or even their ability to continue working.

One lesson from my graduate school experience for which I will be forever grateful is the person-centered counseling style of humanistic psychologist Carl Rogers. Dr. Rogers took *active listening* to a whole new level! In his counseling sessions, he would not ask any questions. He would simply listen while the patient spoke, sometimes nodding, sometimes saying, "Mmm hmm." Every now and again, he would sum up what the patient said and repeat it back to make sure he understood. In school, I thought his approach was a complete waste of everybody's time (sorry, Dr. Rogers!).

What I now know is that there are very, very few people in the world who can handle sitting with another person in complete silence. It makes them so uncomfortable that they have to fill the empty space with words. For example, when a staff person shows up at my office door unexpectedly, my first question is, "What's going on?" She might start by saying, "Nothing," but after fifteen seconds of silence, I usually get the rest of the story. I don't do this to *trick* employees but rather to give them whatever amount of time they need to tell their story and to make sure they know I'm not trying to rush them. Time is a precious commodity in health-care. I want my employees to know they are worth it.

Credibility

Leadership expert John C. Maxwell says, "Credibility is a leader's currency. With it, he or she is solvent; without it, he or she is bankrupt." Dr. Maxwell provides a scenario that leaders walk around with *credibility coins* in their pockets. I tell the leaders I train that they each have a *credibility jar*—I want them to be able to *see* what they have in there at all times and to be aware that their employees can also see what is in there at all times. Every leader's goal is to keep that jar as full as possible, because sooner or later, we will forget something, or make a wrong decision, or misunderstand someone. . .and we will need plenty of coins in there so we don't go bankrupt.

Every time a leader maintains an employee's confidentiality, she earns some credibility coins for her jar. Every time a leader follows through in doing what he promises to do, he earns some credibility coins for his jar. Apologize for a mistake you made—coins in the jar. Address policy violations with staff in a kind, professional manner—coins in the jar.

In contrast, every time a leader fails to return an employee's phone call in a timely manner, she loses credibility coins. When a leader makes excuses (like "I don't have an answer on that yet," when the answer is actually, "no," but he does not want the employee to be angry with him), he loses credibility coins. Let an employee spend too much time in the break room—lose credibility coins. Hear an employee discussing confidential resident information in a public place and say nothing—lose credibility coins.

Earning and maintaining credibility with your employee customers go hand-in-hand with having their respect. It involves being consistent and having integrity in everything that you do. The truth is, no matter how great you are, you will eventually lose some credibility coins—not because you did something wrong on purpose but simply because no one is perfect (a fact to also keep in mind when setting expectations for your employees). When that happens, some coins spill out. You apologize, and then you try to fix the situation (which, by the way, might earn you one or two coins back).

As a leader in a long-term care setting, it is not just the staff that monitor your credibility jar. Residents are watching, and so are family members. Agency staff and therapists are noticing, and so are doctors and ambulance drivers. In long-term care, leaders need to worry about more than just their own credibility jar; their jar and the company's jar are one and the same.

There are a few ways HR professionals, administrators, and supervisors can work toward adding coins and keeping their credibility jars full, the first of which has to do with expectations. A former employee recently told me,

"A good leader is clear about expectations from the beginning, and lets you know right away if you are off base."

I liken it to playing a new game. When you first are introduced to a game, someone reviews the purpose and the rules with you. Based on their instructions, you go about playing the game and try to win. But what would happen if near the end of the game, someone says, "Oh, I forgot to tell you, you can't do that; now you have to go back to the beginning." Wouldn't that make you frustrated? And angry? Wouldn't you want to say, "If I'd have known that in the first place, I would have done this and this and that differently!"

The same is true for any workplace. It is a leader's responsibility to make sure every member of the team has clear instructions, goals, and expectations before they are assigned a task. It is also a leader's responsibility to monitor the team members' progress toward goals and help them make adjustments as necessary to meet those goals. A leader's inability or unwillingness to do these things will cause him or her to lose a lot of credibility coins with their team.

Another way a leader can lose credibility coins is to get dragged into the gossip mill, which is big and mighty in long-term care facilities! It is not enough to just *not* gossip. Leaders must also not be present when others are gossiping and not *appear* to be involved in gossip. I found myself in a situation like this while working in a continuing care retirement community.

After I had worked in the community for a few months, I was invited to lunch by the director of the Social Work Department. We both had a similar sense of humor, and soon began eating lunch together every day. A few months later, the DON position became available, and a few internal candidates had applied for the position. At some point, the Social Work Director made a comment to someone in her department that a particular nurse "was going to get the job."

The next day I found myself in my administrator's office, being counseled because I shared confidential information with the Social Work Director about the DON position. I had absolutely no idea what she was talking about, because the Social Work Director and I had never spoken about work-related issues, especially something as confidential as an internal promotion. Upon investigation, it was revealed that the Social Work Director said she was simply giving her opinion to her employee, but because the employee knew that we ate lunch together, she *assumed* the information had come from me.

Obviously, in this scenario, I had not yet earned enough credibility coins in my jar to show that employee that I would never breach confidentiality. But it was a very valuable lesson, and I remind leaders all the time that they need to monitor themselves, and stay beyond reproach.

Regarding confidentiality, I have one final note. While it is paramount to maintain the confidentiality of your employees and residents, there are times when you cannot promise to keep such information to yourself. Safety always supersedes confidentiality rights.

How this usually plays out for me is as follows: A well-meaning employee knocks on my door and wants to speak with me. Before she starts telling her story she says, "I have to tell you something, but this needs to stay between you and me." Has this situation ever happened to you?

To maintain my integrity and keep my credibility jar nice and full, I usually say, "Let me stop you before you go any further. I absolutely want to hear what you are going to tell me, but if you or a resident or an employee is in harm's way, I will not be able to keep what you have to tell me confidential." I reassure the individual that, to the best of my ability, I will try to keep her name confidential (though many times they are the only witness to a situation and are easily identified because of it) but then also reinforce that if someone is being hurt or could be hurt, protecting that person is more important than keeping a secret.

What would happen to my credibility if I agreed to keep her news confidential and then she told me about a resident being sexually assaulted? I have two choices—keep it a secret (which means breaking the law but maintaining my credibility with the employee) or report it (which is the right and legal thing to do but causes me to break my promise to the employee and lose credibility with her). Both choices are made terrible by my failure to be honest with the employee at the beginning of the conversation. Additionally, if she didn't want me to do something, she would not have come to me in the first place, so I am convinced that most people who lead with those words don't really mean them anyway.

We will discuss the concept of accountability more in chapter 5.

Best Practice Suggestions for Your Employee Relationships

- Keep a computer file or recipe box with index cards for each of your employees to track names of spouse, children, favorite candy bar, etc. (No confidential information should be kept here, such as social security number or birth date).

- Write a personalized, handwritten Thank You note to employees when they have done something above and beyond; attach a candy to the outside of the envelope and have their supervisor hand it to them in their work area.

- Develop and maintain an office schedule that includes spending time with each shift and on weekends; post the schedule for employees to see and keep it consistently.

- Send a card to the employee's home for special events, including having a baby, recent surgery, getting married, etc.

- If your office is in a busy area and you are unable to keep your door open most of the time, make a sign that says "Please Come In" on one side and "Please Do Not Disturb" on the other side.

- When you see an employee do something nice for a resident or for another employee, pull them into your office quietly and tell them you saw it and you appreciated it (I sometimes give a smiley sticker to the person, too—anyone who has gotten a smiley sticker in the past knows how that person got it!).

- Because day shift staff often are the beneficiaries of treats brought in by vendors or leftovers from events or activities, put a case of soda, or some cereal bars, or some doughnuts out for the second and third shift staff.

- When employees do things that make the company look good (giving an impromptu tour, calming an upset family member, etc.), have the administrator or president write a Thank You card acknowledging that they know about what the person did (make a copy for the employee's file and another copy for the employee's supervisor).

- Keep a jar of lollipops in your office, so when employees' children come in, yours is the first office they want to visit!

- Get toys, crayons, and coloring books from the Dollar Store for times when employees need to bring children to meetings.

- Post phone numbers that might be helpful to employees who need help, including employee assistance, domestic violence assistance, medical/health clinics, etc.

- Make sure you say "Hello" or "Good morning," and greet your employees before you immediately begin pointing out problems or concerns to them.

- Do not interrupt an employee's break to ask questions that don't require immediate answers.

- When two employees are not getting along, don't listen to one without the other—invite both into your office, set ground rules for the discussion, and work through it together (don't let it appear, by listening to one employee and not the other, that you are *taking sides*).

- Share the credit with the whole team when there is a success; take the blame on your own when there is a failure.

CHAPTER FOUR

RECRUITING
& INTERVIEWING

*"I am convinced that nothing we do is more important
than hiring and developing people. At the end of the day
you bet on people, not on strategies."*

Lawrence Bossidy

It is my firm belief that a good HR person should have a thorough understanding of each position for which she or he hires. Whatever the manner you use to familiarize yourself with the routine of each job, it will be extremely useful (and make you very credible with your applicants) if you are able to describe in detail what that individual does on a shift. However, as I mentioned previously in reviewing my first job in HR, there is a sense of urgency in health-care hiring that exists in very few other industries. So, while it is important to help on the floor when necessary, and it reinforces that you are part of the team, doing so needs to be the exception, not the rule.

The most important way you can spend your time in support of the team as an HR professional is by filling open positions as soon as possible. If that means an 8:00 p.m. interview, so be it. Starting your day at 6:00 a.m.? Of course! Your team is counting on you to get the job done! And it all starts with ensuring you have a good communication system with your department directors and schedulers.

It is imperative to the flow of recruitment and hiring that HR professionals "have their fingers on the pulse." This means that as soon as a director hears an employee is looking for other employment, you go into action! If it is someone you desperately want to retain, have a talk with them to see if you can avoid losing them—sometimes it's as simple as changing shifts or reducing hours. If you know the reason is something that cannot change, such as moving, or change in class schedules, or retirement, try to get a feel for how much time you have.

One of the most difficult situations for staffing is when someone has been discussing their *last day* for weeks and the HR professional only finds out they are leaving when the employee comes to say goodbye! Equally difficult is finding out on Friday that someone walked off the job on Monday. There needs to be a clearly communicated and consistent method for job openings to be reported as soon as there is an indication that someone may be leaving or has left without notice.

Part of driving home this point with directors and schedulers can be an explanation, including a written document, of the amount of time it takes from recruitment to hiring to bringing a single employee on board. This should include whatever your company's pre-employment requirements are (TB tests, physicals, criminal background checks, FBI clearances, drug screens, etc.), as well as the amount of time needed for completion of each requirement. It is also helpful to be clear on what might prohibit a candidate who seems like a perfect match from being eligible for hire. Having had these discussions with directors and schedulers, as well as giving them a written document to which they can later refer, will help them understand the importance of early notice of staffing changes and the need for patience with the hiring process.

Finally, when you begin as an HR professional in a new role, it will be helpful to get wages and benefits information from other facilities in your area, so that you can assess where you fall compared to your competition. It is a smart practice to complete such a study at least every two years and continue to look for creative benefits to offer employees in addition to their wages. We will discuss other ways to keep the employees that you have—and keep them happy— in another chapter.

Things to Keep in Mind

Recruitment

When I began in HR, if I had an open position, I placed an ad in the newspaper, and lots of people came to fill out applications. Today, many organizations continue to use the print advertisements of the newspaper, but I don't know of any facility that uses this as their sole method of recruitment. When I worked in small facilities, advertising every week, especially the same openings, made me feel and look a little desperate, so I seldom used newspaper ads. This worked to the company's benefit, as more than one person shared during interview that they applied for the position because they had not seen many ads, so they felt employee retention and morale must be high.

Print ads in places such as local free papers may be utilized. Signs may be posted at the grocery story. Radio and television ads are common. Advertisement banners across your computer screen invite you to apply. Placemats in diners and spaces on shopping carts are creative ways to both recruit for and market your company. I have even mailed flyers to local pastors asking them to post them for their congregations to consider.

Posting open positions in-house for employees to view has been beneficial for getting quality applicants, but I also seek out great employees in person to ask, "Don't you know someone?" Many of my best hires were friends of friends who were already employed. Employee referrals also have secondary benefits: employees know that whomever they refer, that person must represent them well. No one wants to be embarrassed when the person they referred ends up being a no-call/no-show on a Saturday night!

Some facilities offer referral bonuses after a new employee has been with the company for a certain period of time. There are a number of different ways this can be administered, including giving a small bonus when the applicant is hired twenty dollars) and then a higher bonus fifty to hundred dollars) when the new employee completes a certain period of time (such as ninety days, six months, one year). I have found that referral bonus programs have both positives and negatives.

The positive outcomes are that employees go out of their way to get as many people as they can to fill out an application (like fishing with a big net—*The more people I tell, the better my chances someone will get hired and stay a while!*). A potential negative impact is that there may be employees who are more concerned with the quantity of referrals than the quality. Also, I have had employees notice someone filling out an application and then introduce themselves and say, "Write my name down as a referral," when they had never laid eyes on the applicant before that moment. If other methods are not working to get people to apply, this recruitment method might be worth the time and expense, but clear guidelines must be developed.

Positions advertised on the company's website are also an excellent way to feature new openings and having an application link can save both time and trees. LinkedIn and Facebook postings can be helpful for administrator or department director positions, but I have not found them to be useful when hiring frontline staff or nurses. While I have utilized Craigslist and Indeed.com, in my experience, there has been very little commitment shown by many people who apply using these recruitment sources. I do get a large number of resumes in response to the ads, but eight out of ten of those scheduled for an interview never show up. I have hired some very good candidates from those applicants, but it takes an extensive amount of time to coordinate and schedule a lot of interviews to be able to meet those two people out of every ten.

If your organization has the capability of utilizing a sign in front of your facility, I have also found this to be an excellent method for getting quality applicants. They are generally people who live nearby, know about what you do, and are willing to come inside and complete an application. However, I do caution that you not advertise your need for staff for long periods of time and with a lot of frequency. Families and potential customers also see that and may get the impression that there is cause for concern regarding staff retention.

Applications

Whether your applications are still on paper or online available via computer, they tell you more than just where an applicant worked in the past. When deciding which applicants I want to invest forty-five to sixty minutes of my time interviewing, I look for the following:

- A stable job history: This means the applicant has spent more than one year at a job. Candidates with four jobs and less than six months at each job will not stay long-term. The cost to hire and train this person is high but the impact on morale when an employee leaves within a few months costs a lot more than money.

- Reasons for leaving other jobs: It amazes me the lack of thought that applicants sometimes put into their responses on applications. While I don't prefer that they lie, it's likely that indicating you left your last job because of a "physical altercation with boss" will keep you from being interviewed at any health-care facility. Equally disappointing are reasons like "fired," "too many call-offs," and my personal favorite quit because not enough hours (which means now the individual works zero hours). I actually prefer "will discuss at interview" to these responses.

- Experience: Sometimes an individual applies for a position that has been advertised, but you know that another position that might be a better fit will be coming along soon. I try to be a big-picture thinker when filling positions. For example, if someone applies for a housekeeping position but they have worked in the past as a cook, I may ask them to interview for a cook's position that may not be currently available but will become available soon. Likewise, some skills are transferrable to different positions. For example, a very friendly and out-going individual with years of housekeeping experience may better enjoy serving in the dining room where she can have more resident interaction. Part of that job does involve cleaning, but it may be more fulfilling for her to spend more time with other people.

- Pay rate desired: I prefer to discuss salary face-to-face with applicants, and many companies have policies that pay rates not be released over the phone. But there are times when an applicant indicates they are looking for much more money than the position is worth. I often call them to verify what they are looking for without disqualifying them automatically. About half of the time, the rate indicated is not written in stone.

- References: Believe it or not, there are people who list their mother and their boyfriend as their references, so I look to see who is listed there (and whether the phone number is the same as the applicant's). I want to speak with individuals who are familiar with the applicant's work performance, not their personal life. Also, applicants sometimes write names but no contact information. If I am interested in the candidate, I may ask that they bring more information with them to the interview if it has not been listed on the application.

- Availability: In long-term care, it seems that everyone wants to work full-time day shift. Sometimes I call candidates in an effort to wish them into another shift, but alas, most of the applications in my files are for this type of schedule. As I indicated above, I may have an individual who does not meet the criteria for an activities assistant position but might be an excellent fit for the housekeeper position, which has similar hours. As a rule, I do not make *special deals* with candidates regarding schedules. Department directors may agree to that, but it is not the job of the HR professional to give the director and/or scheduler more work and a bigger scheduling headache.

Interviews

Each organization has its own method of conducting interviews. In my experience, the HR professionals arrange interviews, and the director sits in. Some directors only want to interview applicants after they have been screened by the HR professional, while still others are happy with the employees that are sent to them without having met them at all prior to hire. In any case, HR professionals should have a conversation with each director to find out their preference and to ensure that if they are looking for something specific in a candidate, everyone is on the same page.

I utilize behavior-based interviewing, which follows the principle that the way a person has behaved in the past is the best indicator of the way the person will behave in a similar situation in the future. For each position, I create an interview form with questions designed to elicit responses that indicate whether the candidate meets or does not meet the criteria of the position. Of course, questions need to be legal, meaning they cannot violate the Civil Rights Act of 1964, the Age Discrimination Act of 1975, or the Disabilities Act and the Pregnancy Discrimination Act of 1978. Those acts state that a person cannot be denied employment because of their race, color, religion, national origin, sexual orientation/preference, age, disability, or because she is pregnant.

For these reasons, employers should avoid asking questions that would cause an applicant to reveal this information about themselves, including the following

- Age: Some states require employees in long-term care to be at least sixteen years old. Therefore, an employer may ask, "Are you at least sixteen years old?" because it is a requirement of the position. However, you may not ask any applicant how old they are, what year they graduated from high school, or what is their birthdate until after a job offer has been made and accepted.

- Information about Family: An employer may not ask questions about a person's marital status, including, "What does your husband do for a living?" or "What shift does your wife work?" Likewise, employers are not permitted to ask about children, including "How many children do you have?" or "That's a pretty necklace; did your children give it to you?" Questions about schedule availability are legal because they are specifically related to the ability to do the job; for example, "This position requires that you work every other holiday; are you available to work that kind of schedule?"

- Race, Religion, or Ethnicity: Regardless of what a candidate wears to an interview, interviewers are not legally permitted to ask questions about his or her attire or jewelry as they may be related to the candidate's race, religion, or ethnic background. Again, questions about the candidate's ability to perform the job duties and work the required schedule of the position are permitted. You may not mean anything when you ask why a candidate wears a turban, but the question has nothing to do with the applicant's ability to do his job and is therefore inappropriate regardless of your benign intentions.

- Sexual Preference or Orientation: Interviewers may not ask any questions on this subject as it does not impact the person's ability to carry out the essential duties of the position for which he or she is interviewing.

- Health Status or Disabilities: It is a good practice to have the receptionist who greets the candidates give them a copy of the job description to review prior to the interview. This allows the individual to review the duties and physical requirements of the position before they meet with the interviewer. It is an excellent way to begin the interview by saying, "Thank you for taking the time to review the job duties and requirements of the position. Do you feel, based on what you have read, that you would be able to complete the essential duties of the position?"

Over the years, I have had candidates for nursing positions who had hearing loss in one ear. One of the duties of nursing staff is to take vital signs, including using a stethoscope to hear blood pressure. However, most companies can easily make an accommodation for an employee with hearing loss by either allowing her to use an automatic BP machine or reassigning tasks so that her partner does all the vitals and she does another shared task. Being physically able to use a stethoscope is not an essential function of the job, so it would be illegal not to offer someone a position if the candidate is able to do all other functions of the job.

My best advice for directors when they interview is to have an interview form reviewed and approved by an HR professional or administrator and consistently use it to interview all candidates. When you ask every applicant the same set of legal questions, every person is treated the same and no one is able to claim discrimination.

Interview Deal-Breakers

Every HR professional has his or her own personal preferences about what they like or dislike during interviews, and I am no different. The following are certainly not found in any interviewing manual, but they are important to me as I decide whether or not a candidate is a good fit for a position in my long-term care facility:

- **Complaining about a past employer:** In a situation where a person should be trying to tell me all the positive reasons why I should hire them, complaining about how a previous employer did not treat her fairly, did things illegally, or fired her unjustly is not a good first impression. This is a great example of why I use behavior-based interview questions. If they sit in my office and complain about past employers, they are certainly likely to sit in another HR professional's office and complain about me.

- **A cold response to "Why do you want to work in long-term care?":** What I want to hear is that the individual has a heart for helping people, or that he was very close to his grandfather, or that her mother was a nurse and she volunteered sometimes. *Cold* responses for me include that the individual "just needs to work," that in health-care a person "always has a job, and won't get laid off," or, "now that it's getting cold, I want a job where I can work inside." I need them to show me, to convince me, that this will not be *just a job* for them and that they want to *make a difference.*

- **Punctuality:** One may run a few minutes late for an interview, either because of an accident, because of construction, or getting stuck behind school buses. I expect individuals who are twenty or more minutes late to call their interviewer and let him or her know as a courtesy. Often, because I book appointments in forty-five-minute blocks, I cannot see an applicant who arrives more than twenty minutes late because it will cause my other appointments to run behind schedule. If there is good cause for the tardiness, I do reschedule interviews, but the applicant should show their interest in the job and their ability to meet the schedule requirements by being on time or early for our first meeting.

- **Attire:** I admit, I used to be stricter about what I considered appropriate attire for an interview, but the world has changed, and I have had to adjust. In the first place, I have found that many people—not just the younger generation—do not know what appropriate attire even means. For example, I think some women believe showing cleavage and wearing a lot of eye makeup equates to being *dressed up*. Some men who wear shorts year-round may think the same about putting on their best jeans for the interview.

While being in the presence of exposed cleavage for a forty-five-minute interview is very uncomfortable for the interviewer, it may not necessarily be a deal-breaker unless there is no room for negotiation. I say this because, with a few exceptions, most of the employees who work in long-term care are required to wear uniforms of some variety. However, I do not miss the opportunity to get some credibility coins in my jar by being very clear about dress code expectations during the interview. If the dress code prohibits facial piercings, and my candidate is wearing a nose ring, I add, "So you will be required to remove your nose ring. Will that be a problem?. Then, just for good measure, I note that I said that on my interview form.

At the end of one memorable interview, I reviewed the dress code with a nurse aide. I explained that because elderly residents have very thin skin, our employees may not have long, artificial, or acrylic nails. I then nodded toward her extremely long, purple claws and added, "So you will be required to cut your nails if you are hired." Her surprising response was, "Oh, no. I don't cut my nails for nobody!. And with that, she picked up her coat and left my office.

While it was shocking to me, I was also grateful that this happened during the interview and not three weeks after I had hired and trained her. Interestingly, a few months later, I received a phone call from the same woman saying that she really needed a job, so she was finally willing to cut her nails.

In case you are wondering, no, I did not hire her. In long-term care, employees need to be willing to go above and beyond to enrich their residents' lives, and they need to do it without having to be asked and when no one is watching them to make sure it gets done. The stubbornness of my purple-fingered friend—to storm out of a job interview because of a common-sense infection control policy—is evidence that what the applicant wants is more important than what her residents need.

- Negativity: Dr. Thema Davis, a minister and licensed psychologist, says, "Protect your spirit from contamination. Limit your time with negative people." Long-term care is stressful on a good day, so an HR professional is always aware of the mix of personalities she creates when hiring, but the price of adding a negative personality to any workplace is always too high.

Take, for example, an interview I had while working for a PCH with an LPN whose only experience had been working in SNFs. When she entered my office and sat down, she immediately reported to me the *violations* she observed while sitting in the lobby. I politely pointed out that because the facility was not an SNF, the regulations were different and nothing she had shared would have been a violation according to personal care regulations.

As our meeting continued, she read from a long list of questions she had brought with her. As I responded to each one—staffing ratios, job duties, reporting structure—I watched her facial expression and demeanor go from surprise to horror to anger. She clearly did not realize all the ways in which the two types of facilities were different. She began to yell at me, stating that the organization was breaking the law, and that she could not believe we were permitted to get away with such things. Everything I had told her about the position was, in her opinion, completely unacceptable.

At that point, I put my pen down on my desk and channeled my Dr. Carl Rogers' gift of silence. At a break in her rant, when she realized I was no longer *participating* in the conversation, she asked, "Well, aren't you going to ask me any questions?. I responded that I felt it unnecessary to ask any questions as it was clear that this would not be a good fit for either of us. I thanked her for her time and stood up.

She remained seated in her chair, mouth open, eyes wide. After a second, she spat, "Well, I have never had an interview where I wasn't even asked any questions!. I calmly told her that it was clear based on her statements that working in personal care would be uncomfortable for her owing to our different regulations. I thanked her again for her time and held the door open for her to leave.

As I have said, employees in long-term care get very close to each other very quickly. What would the atmosphere of the nursing unit have been if this individual was in charge when a family was upset or the alarms were going off for no reason. As HR professionals hold employees accountable for their referrals, employees hold their HR professionals accountable for the quality of their hiring—it adds coins to or takes coins from their credibility jars. One of the phrases I repeat to my team of department directors when they are having a difficult time deciding whether or not to hire a certain individual is "How desperate are you?. Thankfully, with this particular applicant, we were not that desperate!

- Cursing: I will admit that I personally have a very low tolerance for this in an interview or in the workplace. When in a professional environment, one is expected to behave in a professional manner. Applicants who feel comfortable enough to use such language in an interview with a person whom they have just met, in a formal setting, and where they know they are being assessed might also have issues controlling their language when they are frustrated with a resident or with a co-worker or with a work assignment.

Job Shadowing

One of the practices that a number of long-term care facilities utilize is *job shadowing*. After a successful interview, if the HR professional or department director believes the candidate may be a good fit for the position, the individual is scheduled for a job shadow, which allows the candidate to spend some time shadowing with an employee who does the job for which he or she has interviewed.

Job shadowing allows a candidate to see firsthand what it is like to work in the position before they are actually hired for the job. After the interview, the candidate is scheduled to return to the facility on his shift of interest for a thirty- to sixty-minute period (yes, this does include night shift). They are asked to wear casual clothing, and they are asked not to try to assist. This is stressed because the candidate has not been offered a job, and they are not permitted to *work* as they are not being paid.

It is requested that they not wear scrubs so that the residents and family members do not mistake them for employees. Bringing the candidate back a second time also provides another opportunity to prove their punctuality and commitment to the position.

One of the best outcomes of the job shadow program is the impact it has on current employees. Companies are basically asking their staff to provide input on who should be hired by completing an assessment form. This gives the employees a feeling of empowerment in the process. Employees do require some orientation to the program so that they are aware of what they should be noticing and asking the candidates. It is important to choose certain types of employees to lead shadows, namely, the ones who show a great balance of being warm and friendly and also objective in assessing the potential in others.

Questions on the shadow assessment form should include "Did the candidate arrive on time?", "Did the candidate show interest in the position?", and, most importantly, "Would you want to work side-by-side with this candidate every day?" The success of the job shadow program rests on the ability of the employee's judgment in answering this important question. For example, I have had interviews where the applicant said all the right things, but I had a vibe that something wasn't quite right. In many circumstances, the employee doing the shadow is able to identify what the concern is, or at least confirm my perception, and will not recommend the candidate for hire.

While in college, I was a resident assistant (RA) in my dorm. One of the duties of that position was to assist in interviewing students for other RA positions. When I was being trained on how to interview by one of the deans of resident life, she told us that people can be very nice when they are interviewing for a job, but the fact that they are nice does not make them qualified to do the job. She said if we interviewed someone who was very nice but would probably not be a good RA, "Give them a cookie. Don't give them a job." It is not personal, and it certainly does not mean that they are not likeable, valuable individuals—it just means the position is not a good fit. Every director with whom I have worked and every employee who helps with job shadows has heard me tell this story. Often, when I have followed up with directors on the progress of an applicant, they only have to tell me, "I would give her a cookie," and I would know how to proceed from there.

Lastly, some candidates may not realize that there is communication between the employee and the HR professional after the shadow. Employees have reported candidates on their cell phones, asking to leave early, and sitting down with another employee that they knew for the duration of the job shadow. I have had reports of candidates who shared intimate personal information, causing employees to feel uncomfortable during the shadow, or those who complained about their interviewer (namely, me) during this time. Obviously, what is preferred is that the candidate interacts with the staff, spends time talking with residents, and seems friendly and interested in the position.

I have found that in companies where the job shadow program is in place, employee retention, especially in the first ninety days, is high. Adding this piece to the hiring process does increase the amount of time needed to bring a new employee on board, but if it helps to retain employees, it is worth it in the long run.

Agency Staff

Some of my former administrators would be very upset to see this sub-title included in my book, but the reality is that many long-term care facilities find it necessary to utilize nursing agencies to meet their scheduling needs. When I was first introduced to the use of agency staff, I thought it was a wonderful concept—it is comforting to know there is a plan B and a plan C, just in case! Over time, however, my feelings about the use of agency staff have changed (more than once), but there are undeniable pros and cons to their use.

Agency staff are generally very experienced individuals who are available, often at the last minute, to help facilities maintain their state-required hours and provide the necessary care to residents. In many cases, a facility can request that certain individuals return regularly, though this is not always guaranteed. If a great connection is made between a facility and an agency staff person, especially with an exceptional LPN or RN, it may be worthwhile for a facility to hire that person outright by paying the agency's fee for this type of arrangement (which, in many instances, is six months of the income the individual would have generated for the agency had he or she continued to work in the facility).

Use of agency staff is beneficial for large organizations, notably SNFs. When nursing leadership is already working forty plus hours on the floor and when, despite overtime, the schedule is still short on care hours and there seems to be no other option, the availability of agency staff can seem like a godsend.

There are, however, some equally significant reasons to not utilize agency staff, the first of which is cost. In many cases, a long-term care facility pays agency staff double what they would pay their own employee for the same work. Compare this with the overtime (one-and-a-half times the pay) a facility would pay their own staff. This obviously has a great impact on the bottom line. Also, in long-term care, the pay differential between regular staff and agency staff is common knowledge, which has resulted in employees not offering assistance, not providing adequate orientation, and basically giving the cold shoulder to agency employees out of resentment for their rate of pay. The feeling is *Why should they get paid twice as much for doing exactly what I do?*

Without the thorough orientation that regular employees receive, agency staff do not have the breadth of knowledge about facility policies and procedures, nor do they have ongoing relationships with residents that are paramount to giving great care. They likewise have no investment in outcomes, so the quality of their work is based on their integrity as a caregiver.

I have changed my view on use of agency staff a few times over the years. As I mentioned, initially I felt it was nice to have a back-up plan for staffing emergencies. Over time, however, continued use of agency can have a crippling effect on a long-term care facility. For example, because agency staff get paid more, I have seen regular employees refuse overtime and then find work at another facility PRN (at a higher pay rate) for extra income. Staff get so accustomed to agency staff filling in that they no longer feel compelled to assist when staffing challenges arise in their *home* facility. This frame of mind is very difficult to change!

For many years, as an HR professional, I felt that using agency translated to "I can't do my job," and in two of the long-term care communities in which I worked, I eliminated the use of agency staff by over-hiring for various positions. Recently, however, in a facility where even the word "agency" was forbidden, I found myself again considering the value of such an option.

When a majority of employees are working more than forty hours per week; when the nursing leadership is spending almost all of their time filling in on the floor; when, despite a variety of recruitment efforts, no viable applications are received and no quality employees can be hired; when the schedule has more open shifts than a team can effectively handle; and, when resident care is suffering, it is time to consider—as a short-term option only—the use of agency staff (in my humble opinion). Before such a decision can be made, however, a written plan must be developed to rectify the staffing issues (see "Best Practices" at the end of this chapter), and deadlines must be established and held firm for ending agency use.

The time period established cannot be long enough to allow regular staff to become comfortable having agency staff pick up open shifts, and deadlines must be made known to all employees so they know the situation is only short term. In these instances, employees generally appreciate that you are providing them with support and relief but they also recognize that their continued commitment is necessary for excellent care to be provided for their residents.

Best Practice Suggestions for Interview Questions

I mentioned previously that I preferred asking behavior-based questions when conducting interviews. I hope as you review this chapter, you are able to see how these might be helpful when assessing a candidate for the position available. For those who have not used this type of interviewing, I am including some examples of questions I have used over the years:

- Tell me about the time when you went out of your way to help someone.
- Give me an example of a mistake that you made on the job. What did you learn from it?
- What would your last supervisor tell me about your work performance. What were you good at?

- What goals were you given at your last evaluation, and why were they chosen for you?

- Tell me about your favorite resident.

- On a scale of one to ten, how would you rate your attendance over the past two years of work and why?

- Describe a situation where you disagreed with a supervisor's decision. What was it, and how did you handle it?

- What three words would your co-workers at your last job use to describe you?

- How do you keep yourself organized on the job. What do you do?

- Describe your leadership style and how, as a new leader, you get your team to follow you.

- Tell me about a time that you helped an upset customer or client.

- What kind of supervisor brings out the best in you?

- What does it look like when you are on a great team?

- Tell me something that you have done to prove to me that you are a nice person.

- What do you need to get from a job to be happy enough to stay there for five years?

- What have you done to help with shift-to-shift or department-to-department communications?

- Tell me about a time when you and a co-worker had a difference of opinion on a work-related issue; how was it resolved?

- Describe an emergency situation that you were in charge of; what did you do?

- For nurses and med techs: When was your last medication error, how did it happen, and who found it?

Best Practice Suggestions for Eliminating Use of Agency Staff

It is always the best practice to have your own employees cover your scheduling needs; however, if you enter a situation where agency staffing is in use, or if you are developing a short-term plan to eliminate agency staffing from your facility, here are a few suggestions:

- Keep the end goal in mind: it may seem that the road to going agency-free is expensive, but the cost of getting a facility there is less than the continued use of agency. Focus on the big picture.

- Be clear with all staff that the situation is short term, and prepare to celebrate when that time comes.

- The HR professional, Director of Nursing (DON), Assistant Director of Nursing (ADON), and administrator should be involved in assisting with recruitment and interviewing to include on-site, immediate interviews for applicants (which should be advertised); knowing they will not have to wait for an interview is appealing to many health-care workers. Likewise, schedule interviews for weekends and evenings to accommodate all applicants' schedules.

- Overschedule staff by one or two CNAs/PCAs/RAs and one licensed staff per shift (agency staff always go home first), so that when call-offs occur, they do not disrupt the schedule. If needed, regular staff can also be sent home early (someone is generally willing to volunteer).

- Utilize recruitment outlets that you have not used in the past (radio, television, etc.), and have a presence at local job fairs, especially at schools that train LPNs and RNs.

- Ask to present a short training session on a long-term, care-related topic to an LPN or RN class at a local school; bring a small gift with your business card attached, or offer a perk to a student who applies within a two-week period.

- Develop a tuition-relief program to assist new nursing graduates with paying back nursing loans after a certain period of employment with the facility.

- Offer short-term referral bonuses and sign-on bonuses until your facility has eliminated agency staffing.

- As new employees are hired, cancel agency staff; never allow an agency staff person to orient new employees.

- Communicate with administrative staff at agencies and do not allow poor performers to return to your facility; ensure that leaders hold agency staff as accountable as regular staff for quality of resident care.

- Keep a dry-erase board listing open positions in a centralized location so that nursing leadership and administrators can see the progress toward the goal.

- Build up PRN staff by offering incentives for the programs; consider increasing the rates, based on your budget and the competitiveness of the market. If it is competitive, consider advertising the rate.

CHAPTER FIVE

LEADERSHIP IN LONG-TERM CARE

"Leaders become great not because of their power, but because of their ability to empower others."

John Maxwell

I was blessed in the late nineties to have been introduced to John C. Maxwell's book *The 21 Irrefutable Laws of Leadership*. Since then I have become a student and fan of his leadership teachings and recently was fortunate enough to join his team of certified leadership professionals. One of the core beliefs of the Maxwell philosophy is that "everything rises and falls on leadership." With that in mind, I have made the effort during my HR career to not just study leadership myself but also share leadership knowledge with my employees, leaders and non-leaders alike. While everyone may not be a born leader, everyone has the capacity to learn how to become a good one.

Things to Keep in Mind

Servant Leadership

While the concept of being a servant leader has been around for a long time, Robert Greenleaf coined the phrase in his 1970 essay *The Servant as A Leader*. He said, "Good leaders must first become good servants." Nowhere is this tenet more applicable than in the long-term care industry.

The servant leader philosophy has been a guide for me throughout my HR career, and I feel it is one of the reasons that I enjoy such meaningful relationships with my employees. Greenleaf's concept says,

"A servant leader focuses primarily on the growth and well-being of people and communities to which they belong. While traditional leadership generally involves the accumulation and exercise of power by one at the 'top of the pyramid['], servant leadership is different. The servant leader shares his power, puts the needs of others first, and helps people develop and perform as highly as possible."

I have worked with managers who have embraced the ideology of servant leadership and who have reaped great rewards as a result. Unfortunately, I have also worked with those who failed to exemplify this philosophy and who paid the price by not having a cohesive team or meaningful relationships. By failing to recognize the value in servant leadership, managers are sending messages to their employees through their words and actions, such as when they

- develop policies for employees to follow in their everyday work without asking for employee input or feedback (Message: "I know more than you do."),

- walk past a resident's ringing call bell without checking on the resident (Message: "My time is more valuable than your time."),

- hang signs about changes happening within the company without meeting with employees, sharing explanations, or allowing an opportunity for questions (Message: "Do what I say and don't question my authority."),
- fail to attend regular meetings and trainings that other employees are required to attend (Message: "I don't have to do things that you have to do because I am the leader.").

Learning to do the jobs of your employees is a significant piece of the servant leader ideology. It conveys that you may *not* know more than the employees about some things, that your time is *not* more valuable than theirs, that they *can* ask questions or look for clarification on decisions, and that you hold *yourself* as accountable as you hold them for doing a job well.

The disposition of a servant leader speaks volumes to both employees and residents in a long-term care setting. For example, one Sunday morning I received a call from a cook who had tried unsuccessfully to find coverage for three servers who were sent home with the stomach flu. An hour later, as I was pouring coffee in the resident dining room, a gentleman said to me, "What are you doing here? Did you get demoted?" What response does a leader give to such a remark?

Without the insight of servant leadership, the response might be, "We were short," or "I was on call and they needed help," or "That's what happens when you are in charge." When leaders begrudgingly help on the floor, employees (and sometimes residents) can recognize it. This type of help does not increase the leader's credibility as much as he or she thinks, especially when their demeanor gives the impression, "They'd better appreciate this" or "I'm here because I have to be and I am *not* happy about it!"

A servant leader's message to the resident should be one of gratitude and enthusiasm, such as "You know how much I miss you guys over the weekend," or "I just can't stay away from you," or "Nope, I was promoted and now I get to hang out with you instead of sitting in that stuffy office!" The positive vibe of a servant leader *pours* credibility coins into his jar. It conveys the message that others are important and that helping them is something you *get to* do, not something you *have to* do.

One of the phrases I have heard used by those without the understanding of servant leadership is "I shouldn't have to." For example, "I shouldn't have to come in on night shift to meet with an employee," or "They know what they are supposed to do, so I shouldn't have to check their work." In reality, when you are a leader, everything is your responsibility. There is never a time when you "shouldn't have to" do anything – because you are in charge of ensuring that things are done, and done correctly. As a Human Resources Professional, I would have had a very short career if every employee did everything as they were supposed to do, but that would be the scenario in a world where leaders "didn't have to..." (fill in the blank). That's why we have leaders in the first place!

Another mistake leaders sometimes make is to tell employees how stressful their jobs are, how many hours they worked last week, or how they never get a lunch break or a day off. I myself did not realize the impact this had on employees until a nurse aide asked me to speak with another leader about it. She said, "We get paid a lot less and have to work overtime a lot more. We don't want to hear her complaints about how many hours she works!"

Those who are not servant leaders fail to see the value of living this philosophy every day, such as better employee relationships, more trust and respect, the gift of being able to spend quality time with residents, and gaining a better understanding and appreciation of what front-line staff do. Servant leadership allows you to show that you value your employees, as Debbi put it in chapter 3, more than being a body for meeting hours' requirements.

Assertiveness

Dealing with conflict is a part of every HR professional's, administrator's, and supervisor's daily life. Or, in the words of one of my former residents, "That's why you get paid the big bucks!" Any time you work with people, conflict is inevitable because people have different ideas, values, and ways of processing information. Differences have the potential to lead to growth and innovation, but leaders must learn to handle problems and conflicts with assertiveness.

I consider assertiveness to be the middle ground between being an aggressive person, whose priority in interacting with others is to show they are "bigger," "better," "smarter," or "more important," and being a passive person, whose priority it is to avoid conflict and "not make waves."

Unfortunately, many leaders in long-term care struggle with being assertive. They want to be seen as "cool," "fun," "a friend" to their direct reports. They don't want to be seen as "bossy" or "mean." When I train team members in assertiveness, I remind them that an assertive person knows and understands that everyone has rights:

- the right to be treated with respect;
- the right to express their opinions, feelings, and thoughts;
- the right to say no;
- the right to make mistakes; and

- the right to be themselves.

When exercising these rights, leaders must be open—they cannot have hidden agendas or ulterior motives; they must be forthcoming in their thoughts and feelings. They must be honest, genuine, and truthful in their intentions and in their actions. They must be direct and communicate in a straightforward, immediate manner. They must also be appropriate at all times, to never say things out of anger, or to embarrass or purposely upset the person with whom they are communicating.

The first step in helping others become assertive leaders is to help them see themselves as valuable individuals, worthy of the respect of others. For those who are especially passive, I suggest they start small, for example, going to a store and asking for change for a dollar without buying anything. This exercise gives the person an opportunity to push themselves outside their comfort zone in a non-threatening way. Whether they get the change or not is irrelevant; putting themselves in a situation where they can be comfortable asking for something, not knowing if they will be told "yes" or "no" allows them to flex their assertiveness muscle. And because assertiveness is a learned skill, the more you practice, the better you will get.

When supervisors must confront a problem or concern with their employees, they should rehearse in their minds how they see it happening. The location should be private—there should be no audience present to embarrass the individual. They should practice the words to be used, the manner in which they will be said, their body language and tone, and anticipate the possible responses from the employee.

While it may not be easy, supervisors must remember to focus on remaining calm and stay alert to employees trying to manipulate the conversation or press their buttons. If a supervisor does not know what types of things press his or her buttons, it is important to do a self-assessment to figure that out. For example, in my younger days as an HR professional, I realized that a hot button for me was questioning my integrity. During a confrontation with an employee, if someone said that I treated one employee better than another because of favoritism, I immediately became defensive or angry.

It took me some time to finally realize that making me angry was the point, that I was giving control of my emotions over to the individual who said those things. I knew that I was fair and consistent with my employees; why should I let it bother me if she thought differently? I became better at recognizing when employee comments are really just meant to elicit a response from me, and I now am able to redirect the conversation back to the person it really is about. Remaining calm is essential to having assertive communication.

I learned to use *I statements* in my RA days in college and had perfected them by the time I became a graduate student and worked as the assistant director in a dorm of male students. One evening, I looked out my window to see two students carrying a case of beer into the building (where alcohol was prohibited). To confront these gentlemen, I knocked on their door and unpacked all my I statements: "I was looking out my window, and I noticed you two carrying what looked like a case of beer. I need to come into your room to make sure that is not what I saw, as you know, alcohol is not permitted in the dorms." This approach was very non-threatening—"This is what I saw; this is what I think"—and the young men turned over their alcohol without incident. They could not argue that I didn't see what I saw or that I didn't think what I thought. There was no argument to be made.

However, without the use of I statements, the confrontation could have gone very differently. What if it was a case of soda? What if it wasn't them, but two other young men? What if they tried to press my buttons and said that I was out to get them, that I didn't like them? All of these things become irrelevant if I use I statements, because I never said, "You're in there drinking beer!" I said what I saw, what I thought; and if I'm wrong, that's okay, too. I have been wrong plenty of times before. . . .

For example, as an undergraduate RA, I was completing my first building rounds one Saturday evening and heard coins bouncing off the tile floor in a room (for my innocent readers, this indicated to me that inside they were playing a drinking game called Quarters, where players attempt to bounce a quarter on the floor and into a shot glass). As I stopped to listen, I heard what sounded like a large group of people laughing and making comments like, Now you have to drink!" I took a deep breath and knocked on the door.

"I heard the sound of bouncing coins. It sounds like there are a lot of people in there. I heard someone say 'Now you have to drink.' I'm going to have to come in to make sure that you are not drinking alcohol." When I entered the room, everyone was all smiles. I asked if I could look in the closet, and when they opened it, there was a keg inside sitting in a tub of ice. They all began to laugh, which was strange behavior for students who were just caught with alcohol. The resident of the room told me that they had been trying all night to get an RA to knock on their door, and when they filled a cup from the keg for me, it turned out to be *root beer*. Afterward, they took my picture (thank goodness Facebook did not yet exist!), but despite being embarrassed, I had used my assertiveness skills, confronted a situation, and earned a ton of coins for my credibility jar!

Using "I statements" takes people off the defensive. Instead of pointing my index finger at them, I was pointing to myself—what I saw, what I heard, what I think. It is the most appropriate way to confront a person without assigning immediate guilt or blame.

When addressing a concern with an individual, assertive leaders need to state the facts, state the consequences, and then focus on the future. No one needs a ninety-minute lecture about why they must wear a hairnet when preparing food. After ten minutes, it becomes demeaning and excessive. To end the meeting, a leader can simply say, "From now on, I expect that you will always wear a hairnet when you are working with food. Can you agree to do that?"

Often, if I am meeting with an employee who had committed a serious infraction, or if they are very upset about the confrontation, I end our meeting saying, "Let's start fresh tomorrow," or "Tomorrow is a new day." While my goal is to get the employee to comply with rules and policies, it is unnecessary to cause the person to have a mental breakdown. Sometimes people make poor choices, but that does not make them bad people. An assertive leader remembers that and addresses words and behaviors; she doesn't define the person by them.

If your new puppy did his business on your white living room rug, would you wait until next Friday to whack him with the newspaper (or whatever is politically correct when training a puppy not to do such things)? You would not, because by not correcting him as soon as it happens, your puppy will not associate your actions to the behavior you want to curtail, and he will continue to. . .well, you know.

In the same manner, not addressing problems with employees as soon as they occur causes leaders to lose credibility, and an employee is not given the opportunity to learn in a timely manner. Have you ever spoken to an employee about a rule you witnessed him violating, only to find out that he has been violating the same rule in front of his supervisor and department director for months and no one said anything to him about it? It is an uncomfortable situation, where those leaders lose credibility with that employee and with you.

Likewise, leaders must be consistent. They must be and act the way they expect their employees to be and act. If employees are not permitted to park on the grass near the employee entrance, directors and supervisors may not park there either—even for a minute, even on a Saturday. They must enforce policies with all employees, not just the new employees, or the ones who they don't know as well. Being consistent allows your team to know what you expect from them and what they can expect from you in return.

I have not addressed the instances where the person you are confronting is already upset or is becoming increasingly loud, angry, or irrational. Your first move in this situation is to go to a private location, if at all possible, by saying, "Let's find a little more privacy for this discussion," or "Why don't we go to my office where we can speak freely?"

I like the Facebook meme that says, "No one in the history of calming down has ever been calmed down by a person telling them to calm down." While funny, it is also true. Usually, people who are upset have a very good reason for feeling that way, so asking them to calm down is the same as telling them, "Stop feeling what you are feeling." In situations where the individual is already upset when you arrive, once you are in a confidential location, it is good to acknowledge their feelings based on what you observe ("You are obviously very upset about something."). Once they begin, let them get it all out.

In long-term care, employees encounter upset, angry residents and upset, angry family members. Let's face it, in long-term care, there are plenty of reasons to be so. I explain it to my new employees like this: Imagine your life as you knew it when you were in your early twenties, dreaming of the grown-up life you would have some day. What do you see? Do you think about what kind of house you will buy, what your dream job will be, how many children you will have, and what kind of car you will drive? Do you fantasize about family vacations to Disney World, the Eiffel Tower, or the Grand Canyon? As a young adult, all those things are ahead of you and you are hopeful of making those dreams come true.

Then I instruct my new employees to fast-forward their lives, past their dream homes, and fancy cars, and vacations, to the part where all the things they worked so hard to achieve during their lives are being taken from them, one by one: things like their spouse, who passed away unexpectedly; their cars—their eyesight is very poor, they have had a few accidents, and they certainly cannot travel by themselves anymore—their balance is very poor; and finally, their houses, where they made their homes and raised their children for the past fifty-eight years—it's too much for them to clean and the steps are dangerous now. A person may understand why these changes are happening, but could you blame anyone for being angry about it?

I have worked in some of the most beautiful long-term care facilities, but given the choice of staying in my house of fifty-eight years or moving into one little room in a building full of people I don't know, I would rather be home alone. So, when the beans are too hard, the bath towels are too soft, or the music is too loud or not loud enough, employees in the long-term care industry need to truly understand the big picture. When a resident is upset, what he or she really means is, "It's not like my home.'"

Likewise, spouses, sons and daughters, nieces and nephews, and grandchildren do not enjoy thinking about a day when their loved one is no longer able to either take care of themselves or be taken care of by someone in the family. At the point when they are finally willing to admit that they need help (something many families equate with failing or giving up), they turn to a long-term care facility, but their feelings of guilt, sadness, and loss can be overwhelming. One husband whose wife was being admitted to an SNF told me, "I guess this is the end of my married life."

While employees in long-term care are doing everything they can to make a new resident feel welcome, cared for, and settled in, that person is experiencing newness, which is focused on learning and adding experiences to their lives. For spouses or other members of the family who shared a home with their loved one, their experiences are that of loss. An important part of their everyday lives is missing or has been taken away.

It is a great honor but also a huge responsibility to welcome elderly people into a long-term care setting and promise to take care of everything. In a perfect world, no one would forget a document in a chart, no one would get sick at work and have to leave early, and no one would deliver laundry to the wrong room. When issues are identified, most facilities try to find the root cause of the problem and then fix it for the future. That's the mindset of an administrator or a supervisor when an issue is brought to their attention. However, the issue impacts people. And as I said previously, any time there are people in the equation, there is an opportunity for conflict.

When a resident or family is upset, the most helpful thing an employee can do is to simply listen. Don't make excuses. Don't think about what you are going to say when it is your turn to talk. Just be present for them and listen to them. Try to put yourself in their shoes. Usually, if you give them enough time to get everything off their chest, they will calm down. Whether or not they do, it is imperative that your tone be calm and your voice be low and slow. If they are loud and angry, do not match them or try to out-yell them. That will only escalate the situation.

Once there is a natural break in what the upset person is saying, acknowledging that the person's feelings about the situation are valid is a way of showing your respect and empathy ("I can understand how that would make you upset," or "I would probably feel the same way in your situation."). It is a good practice to not assign or accept any blame if it is the first time you are hearing about the problem, only because this is one person's version of the event and you have not had the opportunity to collect all the facts yet (Note: It is usually acceptable to say, "I apologize that we had to meet under these circumstances" or "I am sorry that this situation has upset you," neither of which accepts or assigns blame).

Continue to ask questions to make sure you have all the information this person can give you on the matter and then assure him or her that it will be fully investigated and that he or she will be contacted for follow-up. In order to end on a helpful note, I generally ask if there is anything the individual needs from me immediately; this assures them that I am not putting them off, that their problem is important to me, and that I am willing to do whatever needed to put their mind at ease that the situation will be resolved.

As an HR professional, let's face it, most of the angry people in my office have been employees. As an assertive person, I do not take the words of angry people personally; as I tell my supervisors, "Deflect! It is not about you!" When people feel backed into a corner, they sometimes go into fight mode. In the words of Michelle Obama, "When they go low, we go high." It is unproductive to respond to their taunts, so the best way to handle the situation is to stay focused on the issue at hand.

For example, when meeting with an employee for attendance issues, you might handle the conversation as follows.

HR professional: "Jessica, I asked you to meet with me because I have your time clock punch details, and I see that you clocked in late seven times in the past fourteen days."

Jessica: "This *again*? You know, I'm sick and tired of being picked on! There is no way I was late seven times!"

HR professional (showing Jessica the punch details): "This is what I'm looking at to see when you arrived for work. Are you saying there's an error in your punch details? Did you use the time clock correctly over the past two weeks?"

Jessica: "I'm not an idiot—I know how to use the time clock! What I'm saying is that I never see you bringing Brandy in here to talk about her punch details! This is ridiculous! I can't believe you don't have better things to do, like maybe hire us some staff! I'm working my ass off out there, and no matter what I do, you still find something to write me up for. This place sucks!"

HR professional: "Okay, let's go back to why we are here. Our policy is that if you are tardy six times in a thirty-day period, we need to address it with you. I know you have worked on the floor when others have been late, and that can be irritating, right? So, I am giving you this written notice that we've talked about it and that you understand the policy, so that starting tomorrow, we have a clean slate.

Is there a reason why you're having trouble clocking in on time now—this didn't used to be a problem? Do you need a shift change? What can we do to make sure you are here when you are supposed to be here?"

In this scenario, the HR professional focused on Jessica's tardiness. She didn't take the bait when Jessica tried to press her buttons; she stayed with the issue, concentrated on the facts, tried to focus on what is expected tomorrow, and then ended with empathy and respect. The HR professional remained calm and poised, and she accomplished the goal of the meeting, which was to make sure Jessica understood the attendance policy and that she would be held accountable for compliance with it.

What if Jessica continued with her rant? What if instead of calming down, she got louder and angrier? In those situations, when the individual is going off the rails, I quietly and repeatedly say, "I need you to bring your volume down" over and over and over until the individual does so. Each time I say it, I say it more quietly.

In situations where there is just no stopping the individual, I use what my children call my hand trick. I put my hand out just in front of my body, palm open, at a forty-five-degree angle (not in the person's face, and not like a stop sign—though that's exactly what it is), and calmly and, if necessary, repeatedly say, "I need you to stop" until they actually do stop. This action is not done in a threatening way; it is close to my body, and nowhere near the other person's body. But it is a physical indication for that individual to stop when verbal indications have not been recognized or respected.

Unfortunately, there are also times when the individual is so upset that the hand trick does not help to stop their yelling. In those cases, I have said, "If you can't stop yelling, we will need to stop this conversation until you have calmed down enough to talk." Seldom have I actually had to end the conversation and walk away, but it has happened. When it does, I ask the person to go home and call to arrange another time to continue the conversation. The last thing you want is a very loud and angry employee walking around your facility upsetting your residents and other employees.

I once had an employee's boyfriend come into the facility asking questions about her paycheck. I let him know I would be happy to discuss the situation with the employee, but I was not able to discuss it with him. He became very angry and began yelling and threatening me. Attempts to talk to him and using my hand as a stop sign were unproductive, so I finally had to make good on my threat to call the local police and have him escorted from the facility.

I understand that situations like this are every supervisor's worst nightmare. It is what many leaders foresee happening every time they imagine confronting an employee; but in my years as an HR professional, this scenario has occurred only a few times. Most people who behave this way want to intimidate you into complying with their demands. Remaining calm and in control gives you the upper hand, and best of all, the nice police officer will agree with you.

For those who would describe their leadership style as passive, practicing assertiveness is truly the best way to improve skills. It can also be helpful to sit in on employee discipline meetings and observe other leaders or to role play scenarios with a supervisor before meeting with an employee. Most importantly, remember it is just like building any muscle—the more frequently you work on it, the stronger it will get.

Accountability

HR professionals, administrators, and supervisors have an obligation to their employees and to the company's stakeholders to take responsibility for their words and actions. They do this by being transparent in their interactions, by allowing others to ask questions, and by following through on their obligations consistently.

A few ways to be sure you hold your employees accountable is to see that job descriptions are complete and accurate. The information contained within them should be thoroughly reviewed with new employees at the time of hire. Defining expectations at the beginning of an employment relationship creates the foundation for accountability with your team. Likewise, it is important to be certain that those orienting the employee can provide clear instructions on the tasks that will be required; if new employees see that others take short-cuts and are not held accountable, they will likely follow suit.

Accountability is best understood by a team of employees when they can see that each person's role fits into the big picture of the long-term care facility. It won't matter if the food is delicious or if the dining room is dirty. It won't matter if the laundry is clean or if clothes are delivered to the wrong rooms. It won't matter that there's toilet paper in the bathrooms if a resident isn't being helped into the bathroom when they need to go. Every member of the long-term care team contributes to the overall goal of keeping residents safe, healthy, and happy. Teaching employees about the big picture can help them fully grasp their role in the facility's overall success.

Holding staff accountable for their job duties should never be done through use of fear. A few years ago, I had a supervisor brag to me with a big smile, "I can make people cry just like you do." This statement shocked and sickened me. Good supervisors don't enjoy making employees cry; the point in correcting behavior is always to straighten the employee's path and point them in the right direction, not to make ourselves feel superior.

Employees notice the hypocrisy of supervisors who hold their team accountable for deadlines, policy compliance, and appropriate behavior, but who fail to maintain the same expectations of themselves. Failure to monitor your own behavior leads to lack of respect and credibility. Leaders who have learned this lesson the hard way know that it takes a lot of time and concerted effort to earn back a team's respect and trust after it has been lost. Don't fool yourself into thinking that no one is watching or that no one will find out. Nothing is a secret forever in a long-term care facility. The employees may not let the supervisor know, but it's a good bet that they will share it with their HR professional, their administrator, other supervisors, and any co-workers who will listen.

We will learn more about accountability in chapter 9 when we review "Employee Discipline."

Best Practice Suggestions for Servant Leadership

- When the housekeeper comes for your trash, hand her your trash bag and replace it yourself.
- Let someone who needs just one copy jump ahead of you at the copier.
- Share articles or books with staff who you know have a special interest in the subject or who could benefit from them professionally or personally.

- Remind staff who have just cleaned up vomit or other bodily fluids that they are a blessing to their residents and that you appreciate what they do.
- Respond to every call bell light you see, and notify staff in person if you need their help.
- Set up, tear down, and clean up rooms without maintenance assistance when you are able.
- Respond to "How are you?" with "Great! How about you?" No one wants to hear a leader say they are "tired," or "busy," or "sick," so if you are at work, be positive!

Best Practice Suggestions for Accountability

- Help schedulers find coverage when there are last minute needs by making phone calls or going to the nursing floor to ask people personally to help.
- Complete committee assignments on time and without needing to be reminded.
- Apologize for your mistakes, as well as the mistakes of those who work in your department.
- Watch for signs that employees are struggling and help them yourself, or find someone who can help them.
- Ensure that you yourself are complying with all schedule policies, and that your breaks are within the correct time limitations.
- Go above and beyond in your work, and recognize others on the team who do, as well.

CHAPTER SIX

EMPLOYEE EDUCATION IN LONG-TERM CARE

"You don't build a business – you build people – and then people build the business."

ZigZiglar

Providing a thorough, effective employee education program in health-care demands quite the balancing act. State licensing agencies require certain topics to be reviewed with employees at set intervals. The occupational safety and health administration (OSHA) requires other information be taught annually. Because the population served in long-term care has specific needs, employees must learn and demonstrate how to provide assistance with daily living tasks, as well as how to help individuals with memory impairment, such as Alzheimer's disease.

In order to train all employees, each of these topics, as well as regular new employee orientation, general staff meetings, departmental staff meetings, and others must be done on multiple shifts. Because educational levels and language abilities are diverse, it is necessary to use a variety of training styles. Presenters are challenged to cover the same material each year yet somehow make the information interesting and engaging for learners. Most importantly, the main purpose of employee education programs must not be lost in the shuffle—namely that employees actually learn the information and apply it to their everyday work lives.

Things to Keep in Mind

Employee Education Calendars

In every employee survey I have conducted in long-term care, one of the top issues of concern has always been communication. In an effort to increase communication with team members, it has been my practice as an HR professional to develop, distribute, and post an annual employee education calendar so that each employee is aware of the upcoming trainings and meetings. Additionally, each new employee receives this calendar in his or her orientation packet.

The employee education calendars list all meetings, as well as both internal and external trainings for the year. For example, for Fire Safety Month in October, I invite local fire departments to educate staff on the use of fire extinguishers. Staff enjoy putting out real fires using the department's training equipment, and residents line up to watch the show! Other external presenters may include physical therapists teaching about body mechanics and proper lifting techniques, representatives from hospice agencies providing information on end-of-life issues and caregiver grief, and workers' compensation insurance representatives discussing safety and accident prevention.

Consistency must be strictly maintained with employee education calendars. I have worked in organizations where meeting times and dates changed frequently depending on what was happening in the facility at the time. This practice confuses employees, and adds to the communication concerns. It might be better not to post the calendar at all than to post it and follow it only sporadically. When employees know and trust that posted trainings will take place, they have the ability to prioritize them and plan everything else around them.

The trainings and meetings I lead include a typed agenda, and each employee receives two copies: one to sign and return for his or her employee file and the other to keep for his or her own records. When creating the agenda, I include a statement above the signature area similar to the following:

"My signature below indicates that I have received a copy of this meeting agenda and have been given the opportunity to ask questions about the information contained on it. I understand that I am responsible for the information reviewed, and if I have further questions about these or any other issues, I will contact my administrator, HR professional, or supervisor for clarification."

Written agendas are helpful for employees to be able to review after the meeting, as well as for those who failed to attend but want to review the information later. They also allow supervisors and HR professionals to hold employees accountable. For example, if a policy change is reviewed during a meeting and an individual does not comply with the change, her supervisor may provide the signed copy of her agenda as documentation that she was, in fact, informed about the change. More about this issue will be discussed under "Discipline" in chapter 9.

If all three shifts are required to attend the meeting or training, sessions should be offered on all shifts. For example, if all the marketing employees work on the first shift, the marketing department meeting can be held at 10:00 a.m. But a dementia care training should be attended by all staff, so sessions should be made available on all three shifts, such as at 10:00 a.m., 2:00 p.m., 7:00 p.m., and 11:30 p.m. As the bulk of morning care duties are done between 6:00 a.m. and 8:00 a.m. in long-term care facilities, I have found it best not to hold sessions during these times. Some staff who should be showering and dressing residents might prioritize coming to a 6:00 a.m. meeting instead, leaving other employees to do more work on the floor without them. Or, the opposite can occur: an HR professional may arrive early to prepare for a 6:00 a.m. meeting and no one may show because they are too busy with morning care duties.

While there are plenty of meetings and trainings that are optional for long-term care facilities, such as customer service and leadership development, in my opinion, the ideal employee educational calendar and meeting schedules include the following:

- New employee general orientation (monthly, bi-monthly, or weekly, depending on the size of the long-term care facility),
- All-staff meetings (monthly),
- Departmental meetings (quarterly or monthly, depending on the department), and
- Dementia care training meetings (quarterly or monthly).

New Employee General Orientation

In order to ensure there is proper documentation on file to meet regulations, employees whom I hire receive copies of all federal- and state-required policies upon hire. Such policies, including all employee handbook policies, are reviewed more thoroughly during the new employee general orientation session, which occurred at least monthly in the long-term care communities where I have worked.

It is a good practice to involve as many departments as possible in the facility's general orientation session. For example, the marketing director may give the facility tour and speak about customer service expectations and the admission process, the administrator may talk about the company's vision and code of conduct, the maintenance director may discuss safety issues and the work order system. Reviewing the employee handbook policies is the responsibility of the HR professional.

The length of the general orientation session usually varies from half day to full day, depending how long it takes to review all the licensing and federal requirements. Some communities also offer a second, or even third, classroom orientation day for nursing personnel in order to teach and assess proficiency in nursing-specific skills and required paperwork.

On-The-Floor Orientation

As long as the regulatory documentation has been signed within the required time frame, long-term care facilities do not necessarily have to wait until new employees complete general orientation to begin orienting them on the floor. Some facilities, notably the ones that hold the general orientation session more frequently than once per month, may still choose to wait and have the employee's first day be the general orientation day in order to provide a more thorough initial training experience. However, as mentioned previously, time is not always a luxury that facilities have when it comes to on-boarding new employees.

A helpful way for directors to ensure that their new employees are receiving job-specific training is to develop an orientation checklist using each job description as a guide. Additional sections, including safety protocols ("What to do during a fire drill" and "Where weather radios are kept") and general information ("How to get a locker" and "Where to buy a meal ticket"), can be added to this form, as well.

Obviously, selecting the right employee to train new recruits is critical to effective learning and employee retention. The individual must be warm and friendly so as to make the new employee feel welcome and at ease. He or she must also be knowledgeable about job duties and be able to teach them to another person—something not everyone enjoys or is good at. A preceptor training program enables trainers to learn how to teach *on-the-job* skills. As the organization Learning for Life suggests in its resource titled "How to Teach a Skill," steps for teaching others should include

1. explaining the reason for what is being taught,

2. describing the subject in a simple way,

3. demonstrating how to perform the skill slowly and one step at a time,

4. allowing the trainee to practice the skill at his or her own pace under the preceptor's supervision, and

5. having the trainee apply the skill in a real-life situation under the guidance of the preceptor until mastery is achieved.

When training, preceptors must keep in mind that each new employee comes to the facility with different education levels and experiences and so each will learn at his or her own pace. If making mistakes will help the individual to learn and they do not put others in harm's way, preceptors should allow the mistakes to be made and then correct them tactfully and respectfully. Effective preceptors are positive and encouraging, pointing out their learners' successes and progress.

Regular staff meetings are a beneficial way for organizations to provide a platform for communication with employees, but they also offer other benefits. For example, in some communities, these meetings also include a training session on a topic required annually by their state licensing agency, federal guidelines, or OSHA. Meetings are ideally led by the facility administrator and include agendas as previously mentioned. By prioritizing his or her own attendance at these meetings, an administrator shows that he or she values their time, as well as their feedback, and wants to be a transparent leader.

These meetings are an ideal time for reviewing new company policies, discussing upcoming facility projects, informing employees of new marketing initiatives, offering a question-and-answer period for employees, or simply asking trivia questions about the organization for small prizes. It is not often that employees are together in a setting away from residents where they can speak freely, so it is best to take advantage of this time together. My recommendation is to hold all-staff meetings monthly, but some facilities have held them quarterly with equal success.

Department Meetings

Though all-staff meetings are an excellent way to disseminate information to every employee, time constraints generally do not allow for department-specific information to be reviewed at those meetings. For this reason, each director should hold regular meetings for his or her own department. The frequency of these meetings depends on the needs of each department. For example, the housekeeping department may meet quarterly and the dietary department may meet every other month, but the nursing department may meet monthly owing to the volume of important, time-sensitive information they must review.

Directors may wish to take this opportunity to offer training to their employees during these sessions. Representatives from supply companies, for example, may review chemical safety protocols for particular products used by the housekeeping department. Insurance carriers will offer lock-out/tag-out training for the maintenance department employees. All staff do not necessarily need to know information in as much detail, but it is valuable information for members of specific departments.

Truly engaged leaders may also take advantage of the opportunity to conduct team-building exercises during these meetings. They understand that when a team gets to know each other on a personal level and when they are able to insert a little fun into their work, it can improve teamwork and communication, as well as lead to new, creative ways of completing tasks and solving problems. A simple internet search can provide numerous ideas and suggestions for team-building exercises.

Dementia Care Training Meetings

Regardless of whether a facility has a secured dementia unit or not, every employee education program in long-term care should include regular training on how to help residents (and the families of those residents) who suffer with dementia. The training should include diseases of dementia, including Alzheimer's disease, frontotemporal dementia, vascular dementia, Parkinson's disease, and Lewy body dementia; symptoms, stages, and unique challenges of each disease; and methods of communication that preserve the individuals' dignity and focus on the abilities they still have.

Simulated dementia experiences are a valuable education tool, and facilities interested in offering such an experience have several options. The non-profit organization Second Wind Dreams offers virtual dementia tour kits, where employees and family members can have their senses altered in a manner similar to that of residents with dementia (www.secondwind.org). There is even a company called Opaque Multimedia that has created a video game to imitate having dementia, which they call the virtual dementia experience (www.opaque.media). Such trainings can help others better appreciate just how difficult it is to live with the symptoms of this devastating disease and provide more empathy and understanding.

Other excellent resources for providing dementia-related training include, of course, the Alzheimer's Association (www.alz.org) and the teachings of dementia expert Teepa Snow, a registered occupational therapist with more than thirty years of experience working with individuals with the disease. Teepa has developed what are known as Positive Approach® to Care techniques and training models that are used throughout the world to help families and caregivers better understand the dementia process and how to provide support to those living with the disease (www.teepasnow.com).

Types of Training

There should be no reason for employees to groan and roll their eyes when someone mentions the word "training." There are plenty of ways to keep them engaged and interested in what is being reviewed other than simply handing out a policy and reading it to them.

The format of every training should have a similar structure for learners so that it can have the greatest impact. It should begin with an introduction, which should focus on why it is important for employees to learn about the topic being presented. This should also include what the consequences could be if the employees fail to utilize the information.

It should have clearly defined objectives for learners. I find the best way to be clear is to come right out and say, "This training has five objectives. Objective #1 is that by the end of this session, you will be able to identify the four stages of dementia," for example. As information is presented to employees, it is imperative that they understand "Why is this important to *me*?" If the focus is on "Why the company wants me to do this," it will be less motivating, so examples of real-life situations where the employees will need to use the information are vital.

After presenting the content of the training to employees, presenters should next review that all previously outlined objectives were met. This may be accomplished in a variety of ways, including a verbal review or a short written test, but my preference is to have a few multiple-choice slides at the end of my presentation (one for each objective that was reviewed at the beginning of the presentation) and to have the class answer the questions as a group. I generally take this opportunity, when appropriate, to end on a playful note by interjecting a little humor into the test.

For example, the following is taken from one of my trainings on different personalities in the workplace:

> *No one personality type is 'better' than another.*
>
>   *a) True*
>
>   *b) False*
>
>   *c) It depends on who is in the room when I answer.*

In-person training is an effective way to explain information where it is likely there will be questions and the instructor prefers the ability to interact with the learners. This method can include something as simple as a policy review, requiring little to no preparation on the trainer's part, or as complex as a PowerPoint presentation with handouts that requires weeks of research and preparation. Other options for this type of session include creating a puzzle with vocabulary review words (several types of puzzles can be created at www.puzzlemaker.com) or developing a game where each side of the room gets points for answering questions.

Video-training is an excellent method of presenting complicated information to learners in a short period of time; videos not only require little preparation, but technically the instructor need not be present at all. The best use of video-training, however, includes a time for discussion so that instructors can both ensure that the material was understood, as well as deliver the message of what it means to me directly to the audience. From safety to dementia, an HR professional can find whatever topic he or she desires via an online search. While some videos can be very costly, there are also those available on YouTube that are at no cost at all.

Online learning systems are very popular in long-term care communities and offer some advantages over traditional learning methods. Learning systems such as Silverchair and Relias Learning are able to monitor state and federal regulations and automatically update the information in their systems to maintain compliance in learning. Most systems have pre-developed courses to choose from but some can also create trainings based on information received from organizations, such as their employee handbooks. HR professionals or department directors can assign certain courses to particular job titles, indicate the due dates for completion, track completion, and generate reports with very little effort by using such learning systems.

Some drawbacks to this type of learning are that long-term care employees, especially nursing staff, do not have down time to sit at a desk and complete the sessions, which is unfortunate, because this aspect is meant to be a selling point of the systems. Additional computers also must be made available for front-line employees, but as with other trainings, this time off-the-floor is difficult to find around resident care needs. Though online learning companies advertise that they will save money and prevent overtime because employees can learn wherever they are, training time must be paid regardless of whether it is on-site in the facility or in the employee's home.

Best Practice Suggestions for Employee Education in Long-Term Care

- Ask your insurance company representative and vendors whether they offer training or have access to DVDs, CDs, or webinars that they can share with your facility.

- Challenge your supervisors and team leaders to develop a twenty-minute training session that could be presented to the employees, especially if they have attended an off-site training on a particular subject.

- Create an educational video library program with nearby facilities so that you can share resources.

- Develop self-tests from health-care articles and websites to keep staff knowledgeable on current developments.

- Have books available for employees to borrow on leadership, long-term care, wellness, and other topics that might be beneficial to them.

- Post notices for external training and learning opportunities for those employees who are interested.

- Offer lunch-and-learn sessions on leadership topics.

- Provide each employee with a binder in which to keep training handouts and meeting agendas.

- Hang reminder notices one week before trainings and meetings (in addition to the employee education calendars).

- Draw a name of an attendee at all-staff meetings to win a free lunch ticket, a lottery ticket, a pocket-sized hand sanitizer, etc.

- Begin a book study group with employees.

- Have employees answer policy questions at meetings; the first one to answer wins a candy bar.

CHAPTER SEVEN

EMPLOYEE RETENTION IN LONG-TERM CARE

"Employees are a company's greatest asset – they're your competitive advantage. You want to attract and retain the best; provide them with encouragement, stimulus, and make them feel that they are an integral part o. the company's mission."

Anne M. Mulcahy

Employee retention in long-term care is generally a measure of the effectiveness of a facility's hiring and on-boarding practices, its leadership and management, and its environment and morale. Problems in any one of these areas can lead to significant challenges in keeping good employees on the team. The costs associated with high employee turnover have a financial impact on the organization, but equally as significant, they impact morale leading to a decrease in productivity, the need for overtime, the loss of knowledge when employees leave, and instability of the work environment overall.

No organization can stop turnover completely; there will always be those employees who graduate from college and look for a position within their field of study, those who move to be closer to their families, those who become physically unable to work, those who must leave their jobs to care for a small child or sick family member, or those who choose to retire. Therefore, organizations must find out why people leave their employment and then focus on addressing those issues that are contributing to employee turnover.

Things to Keep in Mind

Hiring and On-boarding

Most HR professionals will agree that an employee's first three days in a position are critical to the retention of that employee. It is said that during that short period of time a new employee decides whether or not they have made the right decision in joining a company. With this in mind, what do your facility's first three days of training look like from the perspective of new employees?

- Are their employee badges ready when they arrive?
- Does someone greet them by name, know that they are coming, and have training paperwork ready?
- How long does it take for them to find out where the bathrooms are, what time they will have lunch, and where to put their purse or coat?
- Are they introduced to other employees, or are trainers only focused on teaching the tasks of the job?

At this crucial time for new employee retention, organizations need to be doing all the right things to show that they value the person and that he or she has made the right decision in choosing that organization. The first step is to assign the individual a friendly, positive trainer or preceptor. As much as possible, the new employee's schedule should mirror this trainer's schedule, including break times. He or she should be introduced to as many other employees as possible so that the new employee feels like a member of the team.

Every employee should be encouraged to be friendly, welcoming, and positive with new people. I have heard awful remarks made by seasoned employees when meeting new staff, including

- "Wait until you're here a while – you'll see how it really is around here."
- "I give you six months!"
- "I hope you can put up with all of us!"
- "Are you sure you want to work in this place?"

Whether they are meant as jokes or not, these kinds of comments have an impact on the new employee and leave him wondering if he made the right decision. Employees need to convey warmth and friendliness when they are introduced to new staff, and focus on the positive and go out of their way to make the individual feel welcome and accepted.

New employees join long-term care facilities because they want to make a difference in people's lives. So, in their first few days of orientation, trainers should give them things that they can do on their own to make them feel successful. Of course, there are things they may not yet know how to do, and certainly if they are not comfortable doing certain tasks alone, they should not be forced to do them. Even at the end of their orientation period, if they are becoming overly stressed because they feel they are not ready to be on their own, trainers should speak with supervisors to ensure these employees are getting more orientation time. But if an individual has shown she knows how to make a bed, it might make her feel that she is contributing to the team if she is able do that without constant supervision. Feeling good and feeling like the person is adding to the success of the team are important to the retention of employees in long-term care.

Positive feedback is important, too. As mentioned in chapter 6, trainers need to recognize new employee's successes; they also need to tactfully coach and encourage individuals when changes or improvements are needed. When trainers are struggling to effectively teach a concept and the new employee is having trouble grasping or perfecting it, supervisors should be enlisted to provide support and assistance.

In long-term care, it is harder to find someone who is sincerely caring and compassionate than it is to find a person who already knows how to properly make a bed. Almost everyone can learn a skill, given enough time and practice, but finding someone with the right attitude is much more difficult. Caring and compassion cannot be taught. This is why, when given the choice between someone with experience who seems to be rough around the edges or someone with no experience and a huge heart, the candidate with the huge heart wins every time! It will initially take more time to train her, but it is also likely she will provide better care, have more job satisfaction, and stay with the company longer than the other candidate.

When interviewing, HR professionals can also impact retention by being honest about the facility's culture, morale, staffing, and any upcoming organizational changes that may influence a person's decision to accept a job. Though this may dissuade some candidates from joining the team, it will save the organization from wasted money, staff training time, and higher turnover in the long run.

I was once hired as an HR director and then found out a month later that the company planned to restructure the HR function for all its facilities over the following six months. This meant that interested HR directors could be interviewed for cluster HR positions—one person would do the training for four or five facilities, another would do the recruitment for four or five facilities, while yet another would do the safety for four or five facilities. Of course, that would have meant more travel, less time getting to know employees, and less variety of work. None of those were what I wanted to do at that time, so I began looking for another position very shortly after accepting that position. It would have been more respectful of my time to have shared that information with me before I decided to join that organization.

Employee Appreciation

Technically, in the United States, Employee Appreciation Day is celebrated annually on the first Friday of March. But, as many of us know, genuine employee appreciation should be conveyed every day, not just on one day of the year. In facilities that have great morale and a motivated, engaged staff, appreciation is a way of life. Recognizing the many ways employees bring value to their residents and their facilities need not be an expensive undertaking, though it does require the commitment of time and consistency on the part of facility leaders to make it successful.

It may seem insignificant, but remembering birthdays and work anniversaries with a card can help show employees that they are valued. Employee events like an annual summer picnic or a winter holiday party can also be opportunities to bring a long-term care team together to be recognized for their efforts. After successful surveys, a pot-luck party with a cake, balloons, and music might be a great way to celebrate. When possible, inviting employees' families to these events can show a team that you recognize work is not the only important part of their lives.

Long-term care employees especially like to do good for others. A blood drive or a canned food or clothes collection might be a way to come together for a good cause. Assembling care packages to mail or deliver after floods or tornadoes can also give this caring group of people a common cause and build a feeling of good will.

Sometimes, appreciation can be as small as the words, "Thank you." As a rule, I always have a box of blank thank you cards in my desk drawer for when I catch employees doing nice things—like spending a few extra minutes with a resident during breaks, or helping a co-worker by doing an extra shower for her, or keeping a list of things residents like on her housekeeping cart so she can make each person's day special. When employees see a leader take the time to recognize a co-worker, it goes a long way to boost everyone's morale.

More suggestions for employee appreciation will be given in the "Best Practices" section at the end of this chapter.

Culture and Environment

An organization's shared values and practices can be called its culture. Culture affects everything employees do in both positive and negative ways. In an article written by CompanyCulture.org, it states, "Culture mirrors leadership. People look to their leaders for signals on how to behave." This translates to whatever an employee sees as being recognized and praised is reinforced for them.

Leaders can influence the culture positively in the following ways:

- Give employees clear, definable goals.
- Show respect to employees.
- Send the message that a work/life balance is important to the leader and to the company.
- Offer cross-training opportunities or career-ladder programs.

- Keep employees informed on renovation projects, management changes, and other important company news.

- Conduct exit interviews with employees to find out why they are leaving, send surveys to those who leave without notice, and then (most importantly) address the identified areas of concern.

- When employees have concerns, take them to a private area and take as much time as needed to listen to them.

- For those who show potential, offer opportunities for increased responsibility, such as representing the department at a meeting or going to an off-site training.

- Seek out and, when possible, put into practice employee suggestions for improvements.

- Complete employee evaluations on time, and be fair and consistent in them.

- Recognize individuals who embody the positive culture of the company.

- When good employees give notice, talk with them and try to change their minds.

- Walk the *talk*—leaders follow the rules they expect their employees to follow.

- Keep deadlines, and insist that their employees keep them, as well.

- Make sure employees have the time and necessary supplies to do their jobs.

In a 2016 study of two hundred and sixty-five pairs of managers and their direct reports conducted by Jack Zenger and Joseph Folkman, the two found that "direct reports of the worst performing managers were also below-average performers. Conversely, managers who were rated as very effective had reports who were also rated far above average." Leaders can—without intent or knowledge that they are doing so—negatively influence their employees and the culture in their company. Some ways they do this include

- repeatedly changing their minds about goals and direction;
- embarrassing or ridiculing an employee, in public or in private;
- talking negatively about another employee;
- blaming the owner, administrator, or other leaders when delivering bad news to employees;
- criticizing the work performance or leadership of another supervisor or manager;
- lying to employees instead of telling them information that will upset or anger them;
- hiring new, but equally experienced employees at a higher pay rate or with better compensation packages than current employees;
- feeling the need to be "nice" and "liked" by employees, and thereby not addressing problems or concerns with others' work performance; and
- retaining employees—including supervisors—who poison the morale of the staff with negativity, gossip, complaints, or passive-aggressive behaviors.

Best Practice Suggestions for Employee Retention in Long-Term Care

- Identify new employees with special, easily recognizable badges so that other employees know to give them extra support and attention.

- Recognize employees who have completed their first ninety days with a photo in the employee break room or their name in the employee newsletter.

- Create a program where employees, residents, and families can submit a person's name when they do something above and beyond; use a point system and give a monthly prize to winners.

- Ask different employees to cover extra shifts so the workload is spread around; don't keep asking the same person because you know he or she will always say yes and it is easier for you. That person will get burned out, and everyone will get used to somebody else volunteering.

- Have items with the company logo (such as lanyards, T-shirts, mugs, socks) for giveaways during special employee events.

- Send high-performers off-site for training, and ask them to present a session on what they learned to managers.

- Allow employees who are transferring to another position to make that change within a two-week period; don't keep them there indefinitely until someone is hired to replace him or her.

- Have quarterly employee contests for writing a poem, drawing a picture, etc.

- Post signs with messages of encouragement and appreciation in employee areas.

- When having special employee events, get a banner made and hang it in a prominent location in your facility so all residents, families, and guests can see it.

- Feature a different department each month for what they contribute to the team, and post a group photo with some information about each person (make sure that all departments are featured throughout the year).

- Before giving thank you notes or cards to employees, make copies for their file, for their supervisor, and for the administrator.

- Make work fun—create a space on your employee bulletin board for cartoons about health-care.

- Invite students from a massage school to practice hand massages on employees; or ask cosmetology students to do free manicures for them.

Recruit employees to play in a volleyball, softball, or bowling tournament for charity; feature team photos in the company newsletter.

CHAPTER EIGHT

EMPLOYEE DISCIPLINE IN LONG-TERM CARE

"Too often we forget that discipline really means to teach, not punish. A disciple is a student, not a recipient of behavioral consequences."

Daniel J. Siegel

No one enjoys doing a disciplinary meeting. It can be as stressful to an HR professional as it is to an employee. While uncomfortable, it is still vital to a long-term care facility that such meetings take place. They enable leaders to be clear about what behavior is expected, reinforce the organization's policies, maintain order and quality of care and services, allow the employee the opportunity to make improvements and get additional support or training, and help avoid lawsuits, including harassment and discrimination claims.

Things to Keep in Mind

Because it is the responsibility of every supervisor to ensure that problems and expectations are made known to the individual in a prompt, consistent way and on an ongoing basis, the employee should never be surprised when a disciplinary action does occur. Supervisors who feel the need to be viewed by their employees as a friend will always struggle with this part of leadership, but it is a disservice to everyone—the employee, co-workers, residents, and the supervisor himself—to ignore poor performance or problem behaviors because of not wanting an employee to dislike you or for fear that he or she might get mad at you.

Company policies should be thoroughly explained during a new employee's training and orientation, and all employees should sign that they received an organization's employee handbook on or before the first day of employment. It is equally important that employees should understand what the consequences are for violating policies. Most long-term care facilities have a progressive discipline program in place, such as

- First violation: verbal warning
- Second violation: first written warning
- Third violation: second written warning
- Fourth violation: suspension
- Fifth violation: termination of employment

It is also advantageous for organizations to include in their progressive discipline program the statement that it is the employer's discretion to decide where the violation falls on the continuum of discipline based on the frequency and severity of the violation. For example, if an employee has been late for work by more than an hour every day for two weeks and the supervisor finds out only when reviewing the payroll reports, based on frequency and severity, she may decide to begin with a first written warning instead of a verbal warning.

Likewise, if an employee arrives for work intoxicated and drives her car into the front door of the facility, the supervisor can immediately suspend the individual pending investigation of the incident. This seems to be common sense, but it is important that the employee handbook support the employer's right to assess the severity of infractions.

The company's code of conduct should include reasonable expectations that are broad enough to encompass a group of potential problem issues. For example, if your code states, "We expect our employees to be honest and forthcoming at all times," any kind of dishonesty can be addressed. This includes clocking in for another employee, stealing money from an employee's locker, taking excessive breaks, or not reporting a resident injury. Organizations should spend time reviewing and, if necessary, revising their codes of conduct to be assured that their vision and beliefs are clearly represented by them.

The Discipline Form

In preparation to complete the employee discipline form, the supervisor must conduct a thorough investigation into the reported violation. This involves speaking personally with those who witnessed the incident, asking them follow-up questions, and getting their statements in writing. It is also my practice to take my own notes during such meetings. This is helpful when submitted written statements are missing information that was provided verbally during a conversation with an employee. In these cases, employees must be asked to revise their original statements to include the missing information.

If there is any written documentation, such as a note in a resident chart or a report form, those should also be reviewed. Previous disciplinary action should also be reviewed, as should signed copies of meeting minutes in the employee's file. Once it appears that all the facts have been studied and it has been decided that a disciplinary warning is warranted, the HR professional or supervisor prepares the form and schedules the disciplinary meeting.

Discipline forms should state the facts of the investigation. For example, "On Friday, November 30, 2015, Supervisor Janet Mitchell spoke with Marilyn Smith about not taking her meal break at the same time as her co-worker. A verbal warning was issued at that time. On Tuesday, January 7, 2016, it was reported that Marilyn went on her meal break at 12:15 p.m. while her co-worker was also on his break, leaving the nursing unit without an aide for twenty minutes." The information includes the date and time of the most recent occurrence, information that showed Marilyn had been previously spoken to regarding the policy on taking breaks, and a general account of what was reported to the HR.

Prior to meeting with Marilyn, the HR professional needs to find answers to some important questions:

- Who reported this to a supervisor, and is he or she a credible source of information?

- Can it be confirmed by others, including the second aide, that Marilyn was actually on her break at the reported time?

- Was the nursing unit really without an aide for twenty minutes? Can this be confirmed by others?

- Where did Marilyn take her break, and what did she do during that time?

- Why might Marilyn have taken her break at that time, other than because she was willfully violating policy?

- Is this type of behavior out of the ordinary for Marilyn?

- Are there other factors that we should know about this situation, such as her relationship with the co-worker who was also on break, or the fact that Marilyn does not enjoy working on the unit to which she was assigned, or conflicts with the supervisor on that unit?

It is a good idea for discipline forms to include an area for the employee to make written comments, as well as a place for a signature. The discipline forms I have created over the years have always included the following statement above the signature line:

"My signature below indicates that the above information has been reviewed with me. It does not indicate my agreement with the information in this disciplinary notice."

When an employee refuses to sign the discipline form, I take the opportunity to remind him or her of this statement on the form. If the individual still chooses not to sign, I do encourage him or her to write their rationale for not wanting to sign in the employee statement area of the form. In these situations, another supervisor should also sign the form as a witness that the information was, indeed, reviewed with the employee. Finally, the individual who prepared the form should also sign it.

Effective discipline forms always indicate the consequences of continued violations of policy. Generally, the statement, "Future violations of this or any other policy will result in further disciplinary action, up to and including termination of employment" conveys the message clearly.

There are situations during a disciplinary meeting where an HR professional may find that, despite the information compiled during the investigation, the employee's version of the story sheds some new light on explanations for her behavior. For example, what if, while meeting with Marilyn, she told me that she was asked by the activities director to finish her meal break by 12:45 p.m. so that Marilyn could assist with getting residents to the 1:00 p.m. activity? During the investigation, I may not have interviewed the activities director as it did not seem relevant to do so.

In this situation, because the employee was told by a department director to leave the unit and return by a certain time, it does not seem fair to discipline the employee. In this case, I would likely explain to Marilyn that I had intended to issue her a warning—that she knew the policy from her conversation with a supervisor in November—but under the circumstances, as she was following the directions of a supervisor, I would not do so. However, I would advise Marilyn that if she is asked in the future to violate this policy, it will be her responsibility to explain to the director the need to have at least one aide on the floor at all times and then to follow up with her direct supervisor.

After meeting with the employee, I would then follow up with the activities director and verify that she did, in fact, ask Marilyn to be back from break by 12:45 p.m. Also, I would educate the director about the need for an aide on the floor at all times and ask that she help maintain compliance with that rule for the sake of resident safety. Despite the fact that I did not issue a disciplinary notice to Marilyn, I would place a statement about the incident in her employee file, to include my conversation and instructions to Marilyn if this situation occurred again in the future.

New Employees (Employed Less Than Ninety Days)

During a new employee's initial ninety-day probationary period, I do not advocate any type of written disciplinary action. My rationale is that if a new person is not doing what we expect her to do, then *we* have not done a very good job (a) training her, (b) explaining the reasons for our rules, (c) giving her the support she needs to learn her job, and/or (d) informing her about the consequences of violating the policy.

If trainers are using the orientation checklist with new employees, they should work together with the employee and with supervisors to identify where the confusion is and provide additional training, if necessary. If the struggle is with a certain skill or in having difficulty with time management, the supervisor may be able to help. Whatever the issue, a supervisor cannot assume the new employee knows what is to be done and is choosing not to do it (remember my monkey story?).

A few years ago, I hired a young woman to work as the sole night shift housekeeper/laundry assistant in a long-term care facility. After a few weeks, her supervisor asked me to find someone else because she just wasn't working out. To find out what this meant, I scheduled a meeting with the supervisor and the employee.

While a seasoned employee had trained her, the new employee told us during the meeting that she was finding it difficult to get all of her duties accomplished during her shift. Once we identified the issue, the three of us worked together to develop a shift assignment sheet. On it, we broke down all of the tasks she had to accomplish in her shift into half-hour increments. This gave her the flexibility to work ahead in an area, if she had time; but she if she fell behind in something, she would have to work that much harder to make it up somewhere else during her shift. Using this form, she was more successful and began to accomplish all her required tasks by the end of her shift.

At times, directors and supervisors might feel that it would be easier to just cut their losses and find someone new. HR professionals generally disagree with this philosophy. By the time a new employee has been oriented to the job, many hours have already been invested into their success. It is unfair for leaders, and other co-workers, to expect a new employee to be able to do everything perfectly within the first three days. In health care, we call this unrealistic expectation eating our young. It is understandable that staff become stressed when they are short, that they are eager for the new employees to step in and lighten their load, but their frustration and irritation with a person's newness can at times be palpable. It explains why some people never come back for a second day!

Choosing the right person as a preceptor can also contribute to the successful completion of a new employee's ninety-day probationary period. If the trainer is cutting corners, you can bet the new employee will, too. That is not to say that she was taught to do it that way, but new people do what they see others doing. Statistics show that people receive only 7 percent of what we communicate through the words we use—everything else that we communicate to them is through use of our voice, facial expressions, and body language.

Supervisors must monitor the work of new employees to make sure sloppiness is addressed, not just with new staff but with all staff. Initially, it does not need to be something for which to issue a written disciplinary action. However, not dealing with the disorder and lack of structure will send the message to employees that either neatness is not a priority or that the supervisor does not care—about the work, about being a leader, about the organization, or about the residents.

What about those employees who were well-trained, who were reminded more than once about a policy, but who have continued to break a rule during their first ninety days? Yes, there are some situations where a supervisor has done everything right, but the individual is still non-compliant. In those cases, I usually meet with the individual to find out what is causing the breakdown. Often, they just are not enjoying the job. Or they don't feel like other people care about the work, so they are just following suit. Or they don't realize that is how they are being perceived. Or the job does not match the person's skill set ("Would you like a cookie?"). In any case, there are options.

If the employee is the type of person you would like to keep on your team but the work does not match with their personality or their skills, you may consider offering them a different position. I have hired a number of sweet, kind people for aide positions who simply could not handle the workload, either because of the smell of body fluids, or the fast pace, or the physical requirements. In almost all of those cases, I was able to find another position within the organization that allowed us to keep the individual.

If the individual is surprised at the news that she is not meeting the expectations of the position despite being coached, I outline clearly what the issues and expectations are and then offer to assist her in whatever way I can to make her successful. An obstacle to helping this type of employee can be that she simply does not see her weaknesses objectively; this can be further complicated by a supervisor who would rather find someone else than spend additional time working with the new employee.

For example, I once hired an activities assistant with the approval of the activities director, yet within the first sixty days of this employee's hire, the director called me and said we needed to get rid of her. The reason, I soon found out, was because the director told the assistant that she was supposed to help with bus trips and the director did not feel what she was doing was helping. Obviously, I needed more information.

I asked the director what she meant by help, and she explained that she wanted the assistant to knock on resident doors, help them get their coats on, escort them to the lobby, assist them with physically getting onto and off the bus, and chaperone them while out of the facility. Then I asked, "Did you sit down with the assistant and tell her what you just told me, or did you just tell her to help?" Her response was silence.

Miraculously, after speaking with the assistant and outlining exactly what was expected from her, she helped with everything just as she was asked, and after that point, the director had nothing but praise for her. I often call meetings where I need to break down information into small, understandable parts hitting people over the head. Many people are not good at reading between the lines, interpreting inferences, or understanding body language and facial expressions. If a new person is not doing exactly what you want, make sure you unequivocally *tell them* exactly what you want. Having the information written down is another helpful way of reinforcing it, as well.

Some supervisors believe that employees act dumb in these instances, either to avoid work or to simply be ornery. It may or may not be the case, but my actions are the same regardless. If an employee is not doing what I need her to do, it is my responsibility to outline what she is doing versus what I want her to be doing and to give her the tools or education needed to get from point A to point B. Doing this makes clear my expectations without implying that she is either dumb or lazy. Her reasons for not performing the tasks in the past are irrelevant. All that matters now is that she performs them correctly in the future.

In situations such as the one described above, I generally extend the new employee's initial ninety-day probationary period by an additional thirty days. This allows the employee more time to show that she understands what is being asked of her and can perform up to standards on a continuous basis. It is courteous to let the individual know about the extension during the meeting, so she is not surprised later and so she is aware of the importance of turning things around within a certain period of time if her employment is to continue.

The last type of new employee to address is the one who seems to simply not care. This might also be a person who had a good interview, but as people got to know him better, some shady things came out. As an example, I once hired a young man as a dietary aide. He seemed very eager to work, so when another employee commented that he was asking co-workers for rides to work during his first week, I encouraged her to give the guy a chance. After all, isn't it admirable that he wants to make sure he is at work on time every day?

A few days later, the same employee informed me that the new dietary aide was asking if the facility had petty cash he could borrow and when he would get his key to the resident rooms. Yikes! In this situation, it was decided that it would be best to end the employment relationship with that individual immediately; if anything was found to be missing from a resident room, it would be my fault for keeping that individual, and it was not a chance I was willing to take.

If as a supervisor, you know you have not made a good match with a new employee, if there are signs such as fighting with good co-workers, disappearing from their work areas, constant complaining about their feet hurting or the type or volume of work or their pay rate, this behavior is likely not going to improve after their first ninety days. While the time that they are employed buys you coverage on your schedule, you pay the price both during and after their employment with poor morale in your department. I urge you to remove the poison as quickly as possible; you do not need to, and you should not, wait until the ninetieth day to make that decision.

Regular Status Employees (Those Who Have Completed Their Initial Probationary Period)

No one is perfect. There are times when a favorite employee is going to make a poor decision. I once issued a disciplinary action to one of my superstars because she had a series of strange things happen in a short period of time (car accident, mother sent to the hospital, slip-and-fall at her home) that caused her to call-off too many times in a sixty-day period. In the previous two years, she had not called off at all! I explained to her that I understood this was extremely out of character for her, that she was one of the superstars, but that in order to be fair and consistent, I still had to issue her a warning. She was not happy (I wasn't either!), but she said she understood.

Would you have written her up? Imagine the repercussions if other employees found out that you did not issue her a warning, but you gave one to Kathy who had the same number of call-offs in that time period. Integrity means doing the right thing even when you think no one is watching—believe me, someone is always watching. Be consistent—it is worth it in the long run.

There are times when the HR people get a bad rap because people think we enjoy catching others doing things wrong and that we relish conducting disciplinary meetings. For most of us, that could not be further from the truth, but I will admit that we see the disciplinary meeting in a different way than most. I believe that most people want to do a good job at work, that they want to be recognized for a job well done, and that they are motivated by people thanking them and appreciating what they do. You already know that I have benefitted professionally when others have shared my shortcomings with me. I believe everyone should be guided toward doing their best, so it is part of my job to share, kindly and professionally, their shortcomings with them.

For employees who are beyond their initial ninety-day probationary period and who are violating a minor policy, such as taking an extra ten-minute break, I point out the issue in a non-judgmental, non-threatening way (usually with a little humor, for example, "Do you have a twin sister, because I could swear I just saw you down here on break an hour ago!"). I may even say something similar a second time, just to be sure they know I have noticed; but I would also add, "You know I've noticed this before, so please don't make me put something in writing." I might also ask if there is a particular reason for the extra breaks, or if something is going on that I should know about. This lets the employee know that the next time I notice, there will be a disciplinary action.

This leads me to a central principle that I ask supervisors to remember: The employee is *not* the behavior. She may have done something ridiculous or said something hateful, but it does not mean that she is ridiculous or hateful; her behavior was. When meeting with employees to issue a disciplinary warning, supervisors are not there to shame employees. Their job is not to embarrass them into better behavior. They are not there to judge the individual as being bad. Their job is simply to point out what happened, explain why that behavior violated the facility's policy, and outline the behavioral expectations for the future.

I have at times needed to interrupt an employee who insisted that the disciplinary meeting was personal. In those situations, I simply point out that it is the responsibility of an HR professional to let people know what the policies are and to inform employees when they violate them. "This is me doing my job." Without enforcement of the company policies, there would be chaos. It is never personal; it is every supervisor's responsibility.

No matter what infraction occurs, every employee deserves to have their confidentiality respected when they are being counseled. Supervisors must find a private location to have the disciplinary meeting. Afterward, remind the employee that the meeting will be kept confidential and that you expect he or she will do the same by not discussing it with co-workers or residents when returning to their work area.

As a rule, I prefer to have two supervisors (or one supervisor and the HR professional or administrator) conduct disciplinary meetings for anything beyond a first written warning. These can become issues that result in a suspension or termination, so it is best to have an additional witness present.

For some supervisors, the worst disciplinary meeting involves an employee who is crying. A crying employee is sending me a message. It can be, "I can't believe I messed up so badly," or "Now this on top of everything else I have going on in my life," or "Now she won't like me anymore—I am so ashamed." To be honest, I can work with all of those. It shows me that the person actually cares. If I get the sense that the individual is crying with the intention of trying to manipulate me or make me feel sorry for her, I simply move forward as if the crying is not occurring. As I have said, the meeting is for pointing out errors or omissions, areas of growth, and moving on.

In situations when an employee is crying (and I do not feel it is being done for manipulative reasons), I give the individual some time and then reassure him or her that my job is to help him or her be successful. I reinforce that I would be failing to do that if I did not address problems with them. After reviewing all the necessary information, I end our conversation with, "Let's come back tomorrow and start with a clean slate."

Most employees appreciate when supervisors get right to the point during disciplinary meetings. There are times when I have felt like the Grim Reaper when I invite employees into my office, so in order to minimize their discomfort, I like to jump right in, say what needs to be said, get their feedback, and then we all move on. The point needs to be clearly made, but there is no sense dragging it out.

Supervisors should not meet with an employee for disciplinary action when the supervisor is herself angry. If it cannot wait until the next day, ask another supervisor or your HR professional to take the lead. As discussed in chapter 5, it is important to know what your hot buttons are and not let staff manipulate you with them. Likewise, when an employee refuses to admit guilt, it is not the purpose of your meeting to force them to confess or accept blame.

If four employees witnessed Jeff saying something inappropriate, you know Jeff probably said it. Your job is to state the facts, reinforce the policy and expectations, and ask him to sign the discipline form as proof that the incident was reviewed with him. If he refuses, because he insists that he did not say what he is accused of saying, you do not need to shine your bright light in his eyes for three hours until he cracks! Simply have a witness sign the discipline form, ask Jeff if he would like to write a statement in the Employee Comment section, and then thank him for coming in to meet with you. Jeff knows what he said, and he also understands that any such behavior as was reviewed with him will mean suspension or termination in the future. Your mission—setting the boundaries as to what is acceptable and clearly outlining what will happen if the behavior occurs again—has been accomplished, whether he admits to the behavior or not.

A day or two after a disciplinary meeting, I try to accidentally run into the employee in the facility. The interaction may only be saying "hello" and asking how the meatloaf was that afternoon, but I do this because I never want my last conversation with any employee to have been about discipline. It is such a small part of what I do for and with my employee customers, I prefer that they focus on the good things about our relationship. I am also sending the message that I do not believe they are their behaviors, that I respect them, and that today is a new day.

Suspensions

When an employee has been through the progressive disciplinary process and has reached the level of suspension, some obvious planning must take place when additional discipline must be addressed. Coordinating with the department director and scheduler is necessary to ensure proper staffing is available on the floor. The time of the suspension needs to be discussed—is it better at the beginning, middle, or end of the shift? If the employee has personal items on the floor or in the locker room, how will these be retrieved? Who will accompany the employee, if needed, back into the facility to ensure that no drama ensues?

Once a plan is formulated, it is best to be as straightforward as possible with the individual. As I mentioned, HR professionals do not like discipline any more than employees do, so I usually get right to the point:

"Denise, we are sending you home under suspension today. It was reported that…, and since this is an issue that we have addressed with you on other occasions, we are at the level where suspension is warranted. We need you to understand the serious nature of this violation. When you return on Thursday, you need to know that any further issues of this policy or any others will result in the termination of your employment."

As with other disciplinary meetings, I assert to the individual that the disciplinary action is meant to outline what behavior we expect from the employee. When suspending, I always indicate, both verbally and in writing, the day the individual should return to work, so there is no misunderstanding about returning to the schedule. For those who truly care about their jobs, it is a humiliating experience to be suspended from work (just imagine how you would feel), so failure to stress that "clean slate" when the person returns may cause the individual to choose not to come back. It is important to provide a way to allow the person to save face; remember, she is not a bad person—she made bad decisions.

Residents' Rights, Abuse, and Confidentiality

Probably one of the most serious issues that long-term care facilities must manage is an allegation of a residents' rights violation. All facilities are required to have written policies on handling such allegations, and failure to follow these policies to the letter will almost surely result in negative consequences by a facility's licensing agency.

Effective enforcement of policies on residents' rights, abuse, and confidentiality always begins with a thorough education program. It is imperative for a facility to be able to show that they take these issues seriously by documenting their efforts to explain the gravity of such violations to their employees. Employees should sign a statement annually that they have received training on residents' rights, including what may be considered abusive behavior, as well as the policy on confidentiality. They need to understand that, if found guilty of any kind of abuse, being terminated from their jobs may be the least of their worries. State agencies may also take legal action against the employee, including revoking an individual's professional license or certification.

It is not sufficient, however, to simply have a signed document about residents' rights and abuse in each employee's file. Facilities ought to review the residents' rights information at least quarterly during meetings with employees. They must post the list of residents' rights and the procedure to follow for reporting any violations. Staff in every department must be educated on what may be considered abuse, as well as the fact that not reporting something can make an employee as guilty as the abuser. The importance of every employee's role in protecting the residents cannot be understated.

In situations where an allegation of abuse is reported, long-term care facilities must handle investigations very methodically and consistently. Upon first receiving notice of a claim, the HR professional and the administrator or the DON must work together to quickly gather information and make initial reports.

While each facility has its own protocol, they follow the same general steps. First, the administrator, HR professional, or the DON meets with the person making the claim and hears his or her full account of what happened. After asking questions and getting the necessary details, the individual is asked to document in writing everything he or she saw and heard. It is helpful to remind the person to simply state the facts, and not add any opinion statements, such as "She was mad" or "The resident was upset." It is more helpful to say that "She raised her voice" or "The resident began to cry." When staff say these things, I usually ask them, "Tell me what that looked like," or "What makes you say they were upset?" so that they focus more on what they heard and saw, and not on interpreting things through their assumptions.

After receiving the initial report, the employee who is accused of the abuse immediately meets with the HR professional and/or administrator, if he or she is present in the facility at that time. If the individual is not present, they should be notified by telephone that an investigation is underway and that they may not report for duty again until they have met with the HR professional/administrator.

During the meeting, investigators should be cautious of the questions they ask. I begin an interview in these situations like this:

"Natalie, we received a report that Mrs. Jenkins was very upset after you assisted her with care this morning. Can you tell us what happened?"

Notice I did not say, "Did you abuse Mrs. Jenkins this morning?" or "Miranda told us you were abusive to a resident today." As you advised the individual who reported the incident, it is your job to only state what you know (through what was seen and what was heard), not to interpret intentions or assume how others felt. As the employee shares her version of the events, ask questions and get as many details as possible. Some questions might include

- Were you upset about anything when you were assisting Mrs. Jenkins?

- Do you recall saying anything that may have been abrupt or upsetting to the resident?
- Did you raise your voice. How would you describe your tone when you spoke with her?
- Tell us about what you said and did when you were alone with Mrs. Jenkins.
- Were any other employees with you while you were in Mrs. Jenkins' room. What did they do or say while they were in there?
- Did the resident become upset while you were in the room. If so, why?
- What did you do when the resident became upset?

These questions do not assume guilt or wrong-doing. They are simply asked so that investigators can develop a picture of the scenario as it occurred. After all questions have been answered, investigators should have the employee write a thorough description of everything she shared. This should be followed by reviewing the process with her, which includes sending the employee home under suspension until the investigation is complete and necessary actions are reviewed with the administrative team. Some HR professionals also include information about notifying the resident's family, the state licensing agency, and the area office of aging during this meeting, as well.

When suspending someone in these situations, my version of what is said sounds something like this:

"As you know, we take all abuse allegations very seriously. So, in order to thoroughly review all the aspects of this situation,

we need to take you off the schedule until we have had the opportunity to investigate. We will be talking to the resident, as well as to staff; is there anyone with whom you suggest we speak to get more information on this incident?"

Removing an individual from her work schedule is done as a protection for the residents. If, at the end of your investigation, it is felt that the employee was abusive toward the resident, allowing the individual to continue to work while you investigate will put the other residents at risk. The employee will most likely be very upset or very angry or both. Supervisors should assure her that there is no presumption of guilt, that they will look at all the information objectively and get back to her as soon as they have collected and reviewed everything.

When gathering information, investigators will need to meet with each employee who worked with the individual during the shift. Some may have nothing to add to the investigation, in which case I always have them put that statement in writing ("Today I worked with Natalie. I did not see or hear anything unusual when we worked together."). Questions to ask other employees are equally important and should be similar to those asked of the employee being investigated. Supervisors should not say or imply that abuse took place; they should only ask for what was seen and heard by those who were in the area at the time. Additionally, each employee should be told that the investigation is confidential, and they may not discuss any of the information with other employees or residents. Likewise, if the suspended employee asks for the name of the person who made the initial claim, I generally respond with "I am not able to share that information with you."

Speaking with residents can be challenging, especially if they have a diagnosis of dementia, if they are non-verbal, if they have difficulty hearing or understanding the language you are using, or if they do not want to get an employee in trouble. As with others who have provided testimony, supervisors should not imply that abuse occurred; they should simply ask questions, such as

- How is your day going? Did anything unusual happen today?
- I heard you had a rough morning today; can you tell me what happened?
- Did someone upset you?
- Were you feeling okay this morning when staff came to help you get dressed?
- Did everyone treat you okay today?
- What do you think about the folks who come to help you? Do they do a good job?
- Are you afraid of anything here? Do you feel safe?

After all the statements have been reviewed, the administrator and HR professional must decide if the abuse did, in fact, occur. If they believe that it did, they must also decide the appropriate course of action necessary for discipline. I have found there to be four outcomes of an abuse investigation.

First, the individual may provide a plausible explanation for what occurred, which was not considered to be abusive and which the resident corroborates. In these cases, the individual is returned to duty and paid for the time for which she was suspended. Unfortunately, this is not a common outcome. Equally uncommon is the second scenario where the employee comes right out and admits to abusing the resident. Obviously, in such situations the employee is released from employment immediately.

Much more frequently, a scenario occurs where the employee behaved unprofessionally. A situation comes to mind of an aide who did not have much experience working with the elderly, and a resident reported that she was verbally abusive to her. Upon investigation, it was determined that the employee had asked the resident to move her "butt" to the edge of the bed. It was unclear what the individual's tone was when she made the request, but the resident was more offended by the word "butt" than by the way the employee said the words. So, the ultimate question for the investigators came down to whether or not calling someone's bottom their butt was abusive.

Many things were considered in this scenario, including that the employee had not had much experience, that she did not believe she was being disrespectful, that she did not realize that the resident was offended by her use of the word, and that other residents were not as sensitive to the word as that particular resident had been. Ultimately, in this situation, we gave the employee a written warning and a suspension and educated her on appropriate terminology for working with seniors. We also changed her assignment so that she would not be providing care to the resident whom she had upset.

Whenever an abuse investigation occurs and the outcome is determined to be a written warning with suspension, I make sure employees understand that in these types of situations, no one ever gets more than one chance. The rationale is simple: If I send my licensing agency an abuse investigation report with Natalie's name on it and, after investigation, decide to retain that employee stating that I will re-train her, what do you suppose might happen if I send another abuse investigation report with Natalie's name on it two months later? My licensing agency may question whether or not I am keeping residents safe. At that point, keeping Natalie becomes a liability for my long-term care facility and my residents.

The final scenario is one that occurs when the resident is unable to provide credible testimony that something occurred, and investigators must make a decision whether or not they believe the incident really happened. As indicated, many pieces of information will play into the decision to keep or terminate the employee, including previous disciplinary actions, evaluations, overall attitude, etc. This is the most difficult decision to make and is also, unfortunately, the most common scenario I have encountered when investigating an abuse allegation.

Best Practice Suggestions for Employee Discipline in Long-Term Care

- Ensure that you have all new employees sign a form that they have received an employee handbook upon hire.

- Maintain a file of all discipline forms for each employee in a central location; directors may keep copies in a secured location, but they should not have the only, original copy.

- Make sure leaders know and understand how to implement your progressive discipline policy, including that they may never immediately terminate someone.

- Employees should never be surprised with a first or a second written warning.

- Supervisors must be willing to do whatever it takes to make employees successful, including creating forms to help them stay organized or spending extra time training them.

- Go overboard training employees on residents' rights, abuse, and confidentiality.
- Never underestimate the value of keeping notes during employee meetings; such documentation is vital to successful unemployment claims and other legal proceedings.

Chapter Nine

Employee Terminations in Long-Term Care

"In the middle of every difficulty lies opportunity."

Albert Einstein

Usually when people find out what I do, their first question is something like, "Oh! How can you live with yourself, firing all those people?"

I am hopeful that you have a clearer understanding after reading the previous chapters that I see the focus of my job in HR being to hire excellent employees and to find ways to keep them happy and productive. In long-term care, it is also my goal to make sure residents in my facilities are well cared-for and safe and that the organization is successful.

There are those unfortunate times, however, when residents are not getting what they need, when they are not being kept safe, or when an employee is being unproductive. There are times when an employee is unhappy—with their job duties, their work environment, or the people with whom they work. There are times when, despite the efforts of the supervisors, HR professionals, and the employee himself, the job is simply not the right fit for the individual. In those situations, it is best for everyone involved if the failing relationship is brought to an end.

Many years ago, I asked a young employee to come and see me in my office. When she came in, she was literally shaking! I asked her what was wrong, and she anxiously said, "I'm so scared! Am I getting fired?" I explained to her as I have explained to many employees over the years, "If I am going to fire you, you will see it coming like a Mack Truck." Of course, if you have done something egregious, like assaulting someone or setting the building on fire, you should expect to be terminated from employment (without any prior warnings!). But, in the normal course of business, HR professionals do not just decide one day, "I've had enough of Brianna—let's set her loose today!"

This topic seems to be one of the most misunderstood in HR, so let's look at some important aspects of terminating employees in long-term care.

Things to Keep in Mind

Illegal Reasons to Fire Employees

Most states in the United States are considered at-will employment states. This means that companies may end someone's employment whenever they please for any reason or for no reason as long as it is not illegal. Illegal reasons include the following:

- Discrimination: By federal law, employers cannot terminate a person's employment because of their race, gender, national origin, physical or mental disability, religion, genetic information, or their age (if the person is forty or older). It is also discrimination to terminate someone from employment because they are pregnant or because they have a medical condition related to pregnancy or childbirth.

Employers should be cautious when they are in situations where it is necessary to eliminate positions or lay people off. If all those whose positions are being terminated are in a protected class (over the age of forty, for example) and no employees under the age of forty are impacted, you will need to have very good reasons documented for your decisions (and, my recommendation would be to consult with your lawyer first). There may be absolutely no merit to a case, but it is nonetheless expensive for a company to have legal action brought against them and have to defend their decisions, regardless of whether or not they did anything wrong.

Because long-term care employees are overwhelmingly female, I would also like to add a note about pregnancy. You may not refuse to hire an individual who is pregnant if she is able to perform the essential duties of the job and successfully completes all pre-employment requirements. You may also not terminate an employee because of her pregnancy. The individual is eligible for FMLA leave (which protects her job for a period of at least twelve weeks) if she has been an employee for more than one year and has met the requirement of working one thousand two hundred fifty hours in that time. FMLA leave must be granted by employers who have more than fifty employees working within a seventy-five-mile radius.

In many but not all states, it is also illegal to fire someone because of their sexual orientation and their marital status.

- Retaliation: It is illegal to fire an employee for asserting his or her rights under state and federal antidiscrimination laws.

This includes not just terminating his or her employment but any unfavorable action that you (or one of your employees) take against an employee because that individual complained about harassment or discrimination. It is viewed as retaliation if what is done to the employee is interpreted as being done to show the other employees, "This is what happens when you complain about the company."

Also in this category, employees cannot be punished for providing verbal or written statements to any agencies, such as OSHA or the department of labor, who might be investigating claims against the company. Punishment or unfavorable actions, called adverse action in legalese, can include being demoted, disciplined, having pay decreased, receiving a negative evaluation, having job duties or shift hours changed, or being terminated from employment. It can also be considered an adverse action if an individual is subjected to hostile words or behaviors by other employees because of their actions.

Again, I suggest thorough and copious notes in situations where individuals register complaints. I have been in a situation where a new employee did not fully understand the regulations for a PCH and registered complaints with the administration because the facility was violating regulations (though the regulations she was quoting applied only to Skilled Care Facilities, not to PCHs). She was causing an uproar on the nursing floor, in front of residents, staff, and family members, so I asked her to meet with me before the next time she was scheduled to work. At first the employee expressed appreciation that I had reached out to her.

However, when she failed to keep that appointment and refused all my efforts to schedule another, I asked the scheduler to not put her back on the schedule (she was a PRN employee) until she and I could meet and resolve the concerns she had had. The notice the company later received from her lawyer stated that the company harassed her and retaliated against her for reporting violations. Despite the fact that the employer's case was strong and, had it gone to trial, the employer likely would have won, this issue was settled out of court. Going to trial costs an employer attorney fees, settlement money, time, and potentially its reputation—whether or not any wrongdoing has occurred.

To avoid these types of situations, it is imperative to follow policy to the letter, document meetings with employees, explain consequences for failing to follow protocols, and take all complaints seriously. Doing these things shows an employer's good faith efforts to provide the best services to its residents.

- Complaints about Occupational Safety and Health Violations: If an employee complains that the work environment or working conditions violate state or federal health and safety requirements, organizations may not legally terminate that individual's employment for this reason.

- Alien Status: If an employee is legally eligible to work in the United States, it is illegal to terminate his or her employment owing to their alien status.

- Refusal to Take a Lie Detector Test: Lie detector tests, or polygraphs, are not considered reliable and are not admissible in court. It is illegal to be terminated from employment for refusing to submit to such a test.

- Company Not Following Its Own Established Policies for Termination: When an employer fails to follow its own protocols and terminates an employee, the company can be sued for wrongful termination. This should be especially concerning to HR professionals and administrators who might allow directors and supervisors the authority to terminate their own employees. It is imperative for legal reasons that an employer's termination practices are followed consistently as they are written.

In one of my positions, when I began with the company, the employees in the dietary department referred to it as Hell's Kitchen. This was mainly because the director of that department fired people indiscriminately with no regard for the progressive discipline policy. I found this out the hard way when I went looking for an employee and was told that the director had gotten mad and fired her that morning.

When I later met with that director, I tried to explain the importance of both the company's discipline protocols and the responsibilities of an HR professional (as I was the first person to hold that position with the company). His response ("This is my kitchen and I'll fire whoever I want!") was proof that he was unable or unwilling to conduct business in a professional, legal manner.

One final legal issue to review involves giving employee references after someone's employment has ended. Employer representatives—supervisors, directors, HR professionals, and administrators—can put their facility in a situation of being held liable for misrepresentation or defamation if the information provided results in the individual not being offered that job.

It is best practice to have all reference requests handled through the HR department and to only verify dates, job title, and employment location for former employees. Even then, I only provide that information after receiving a signed release of liability form. As you can see, it is imperative that all supervisors know and understand the reasons for not providing random reference information on former employees. They need to consistently follow the company's protocols when they receive that reference call.

How to Prepare for Termination Meetings

Once the decision has been made to end an individual's employment, there are things that an HR professional must prepare, beginning with setting the day and time for the meeting. This must be coordinated within the department for staffing coverage and can be tricky, as you may need to ask other employees to cover a shift that technically is not yet open. There may be questions as other employees attempt to figure out what is going on. Remember to always maintain confidentiality (I suggest, "Sorry, I'm not able to discuss it.").

Employees deserve to meet face-to-face with the individuals who are terminating them—this is not a conversation for the telephone. It is usually best if an employee is let go at the beginning of his or her shift; terminating an employee at the end of a shift when she and other employees will be exiting the building together can be a very bad idea. Some employers follow up termination meetings with an official letter sent to the employee's home address, thereby providing the employee with written documentation of the termination.

It is best practice to have two representatives present during termination meetings so that, if needed for a hearing, there is a witness to corroborate the testimony. The HR professional should have copies of the employee's previous discipline forms available during the meeting to be able to reinforce to the individual that the employer's progressive discipline program has been followed.

It should be decided ahead of time who will lead the termination meeting and what will be said. This should include information about continued insurance, such as cost, how to pay, whom to contact with questions, etc. It is important to be able to answer any of the individual's questions about benefit time (vacation days, sick days), if and how it will be paid, and when and how the person can expect a final paycheck.

Those present for a termination meeting should be prepared for a range of emotions from anger to embarrassment to completely falling apart. You should always keep in mind that your actions are not personal and have nothing to do with whether or not the employee is nice or good. Someone can certainly be a good person but not be a good fit for the organization.

The Termination Meeting

Getting to the point of the meeting when you are terminating an employee is appreciated by everyone. If you have followed progressive discipline, the employee will not be surprised by his or her visit to the office, and the termination meeting is not about making the individual feel bad, feel guilty, or feel like a failure. Your goal during this meeting is to end the employment relationship by focusing on facts and provide the individual with his or her dignity. The meeting should take no more than ten to fifteen minutes.

Here is an example of how I might start a termination meeting:

"Thank you for coming to meet with us, Leanna. Unfortunately, we are letting you go today. As you know, we have been discussing your work performance and the issues you have had getting along with co-workers for quite a few months.

Over the weekend it was reported by three employees including a supervisor that you yelled at a co-worker in front of the residents and some family members. Because we have met several times already—I have a copy of your last disciplinary warning where you were suspended for this type of behavior— unfortunately, today is your last day with us.

"Your last paystub will be mailed to you by certified mail, and your remaining vacation time, which is three days, will be paid out to you on that check. When anyone requests a reference, we will only verify dates of employment and job title—we will not disclose the reason for your termination.

"Thank you for helping us take care of our residents. It may not have worked out, but we do appreciate what you have contributed while you were with us.

"At this point, I will need you to turn in your keys and badge. I will ask that you calmly collect your things and leave the building—we will not be discussing your absence with anyone other than to say that you are not here. Do you have any questions before you go?"

If the individual wants to debate why he or she should not be let go or if they want to give their point of view regarding what happened over the weekend, I generally will say something like:

"Leanna, I hear what you are saying, but we were very clear the last time we met that if anything else occurred, your position would be terminated. I have statements from a number of people who witnessed the incident over the weekend, and you

are welcome to add your comments to the discipline form. However, the decision to terminate your employment has already been made and is final."

If Leanna states that she needs to get some personal items from the facility or that she would like to say goodbye to some people before she leaves, I might say,

"Where do you have your personal items and what are they. We can ask the DON to go to the floor and get them for you. Unfortunately, I am going to ask that you not go back into the facility, per our handbook policy."

If Leanna raises her voice, begins to tell you what she really thinks of you, and why this place is going down the toilet, I might respond calmly and respectfully like this:

"Okay, it sounds like this wasn't working for either of us, so what I will ask you to do is immediately leave the property. I understand that you are upset, but we cannot have your behavior upsetting the residents."

The individual may yell all the way out of the facility (with an escort physically walking behind her—though not too closely—to ensure that she leaves without further incident). However, if Leanna refuses to leave the property, I ask another employee—loudly enough so that Leanna can hear me—to call the local police and notify them that we have an individual who needs to be removed from the building. These types of occurrences happen very infrequently, though they are the stuff of supervisors' nightmares. You need to have your plan ready, and be calm and respectful at all times. Do not lose your dignity just because the individual is losing hers.

Sometimes I am asked, "What can we do if residents see this?" I remind people that residents in long-term care have been nurses, managers, employees, or business owners themselves and they are not always as fragile as we may think when it comes to situations like this—many of them may have seen far worse! We can later apologize to them for having had to witness the incident, but the reality is that the terminated employee made herself look unprofessional through her own actions.

What could be worse than being yelled at throughout the facility by a disgruntled terminated employee? How about if the employee begins to cry and is unable to stop or speak while you are meeting with her? Generally, I give the individual a few minutes, during which time I don't say anything. This is difficult, and minutes will seem like hours when all you are doing is waiting for a person to stop crying, but I think of it like this: I admire that a person cares enough about their job (at least she does while she is sitting in front of me) to have this kind of emotional response. So, in order to give this person her dignity, I will let her fall apart, let her put herself back together, and then assure her that there is another position out there in the world that will be a better fit for her.

In all the years in which I have done employee terminations, not once have I ever said the words, "You're fired." They are unkind words, and there's no reason for them. Even in situations when the person you are letting go has been a thorn in your side, when she has argued with you at every turn, when she has gossiped about you with the staff, and reported lies about you to your supervisor, as an

HR professional, no matter how hard an employee tries to make it personal, it is never personal; it's never about *you*.

For those of you who are still terrified of terminating someone's employment, I would like to share my best termination story—the story of Joseph. Joseph was sponsored by a church to come from Kenya to the United States, and I first hired him to work in my facility's laundry department. He was a sweet, kind, hardworking young man who was very appreciative of the opportunities that had been given to him, and he took his job very seriously. . .at first.

You see, Joseph was in his early twenties at that time, and, as I mentioned, he was a wonderful young man. As his circle of friends expanded, so did his social calendar. Late night partying became a frequent activity, and he found it harder and harder to get to work on time in the morning. After a few incidents, I met with him to discuss the reasons for the attendance issues and to offer him a change in shift, which he gratefully accepted after apologizing for letting me down and promising to get back on the straight and narrow.

Unfortunately, though, a different shift did not solve Joseph's problems, and he began to miss work completely. In meeting with him again, he shared more information with me about his busy social life and was again apologetic and promised to improve. I provided him with a reality check, namely, "If this continues, the consequences will be..."

A few weeks later, Joseph was a no-call/no-show for his shift, and I had to meet with him to terminate his employment. He was, of course, upset but said he understood the decision. You might be thinking, "That's it? How is that her best termination story?" It is the best because of what happened three years later.

In the three years that followed, I had changed positions, moving from a continuing care retirement community in Lancaster, Pennsylvania, to a facility in Harrisburg, Pennsylvania (roughly forty miles away), which was owned by one of the largest long-term care corporations in the country. One evening, I attended an HR conference held at a hotel in Harrisburg with many of my cohorts from the corporation's other facilities. As we were served our meal, I recognized the gentleman who filled my water glass as Joseph!

When I greeted him by name, a huge smile spread across his face. He said, "Miss Lori, could I ask that you please stand up so I may hug you?" Of course, I obliged, and after that hug he thanked me for trying to help him, and expressed his *appreciation* for my terminating his employment. He said he was on the wrong path and involved with the wrong people, and losing that job was a major turning point in his life. Afterward, he had moved to Harrisburg and started over. He said he now was successful and happy, and he thanked God for putting me in his life at the right time and telling him what he needed to hear to make that change.

Joseph was a unique young man, and it is likely that few, if any, of the individuals whom you terminate from employment will be thanking you, but I tell you this story to encourage you. Most people appreciate clear boundaries, and when they are crossed, they appreciate the consistency of consequences. Some enlightened individuals might even be able to see beyond what you have taken away, to what you have given them.

Best Practice Suggestions for Employee Terminations in Long-Term Care

- Not dealing with an employee who harasses others or who creates a hostile work environment can create bigger legal issues for an organization.

- Be cautious of your facial expressions when you terminate someone's employment; you want to appear serious but not angry and not seemingly happy. Practice in front of a mirror, if necessary.

- Before terminating individuals who seem to have a short fuse, role play with the person who will be sitting in as your witness. Practice the worst case scenario, so if it occurs, you are prepared. You may want to have a security guard in the vicinity, just in case you need additional support.

- Plan ahead of time who will be going to the floor to pick up the employee's belongings; have the director do reconnaissance to see what the employee brings to the floor when they arrive.

- If an employee asks if they would be permitted to resign instead of being fired, hand them a tablet and pen and get this in writing before they leave. Some people do this so it is not on their record that they were terminated from a job; however, if an employee terminates his own employment, it is more difficult for that individual to receive unemployment compensation benefits.

- If an individual asks about unemployment eligibility, explain that eligibility for this is determined by the Unemployment Office. If she applies for unemployment compensation benefits, she will have to provide her version of why she was terminated from employment, and the employer will provide its version. I usually tell people who ask.

"We feel confident that we followed our protocols and that termination was warranted, so we would contest your request for those benefits; but it is ultimately up to the people at the Unemployment Office to make the decision."

- Say, "Your employment *has been* terminated," not "Your employment *will be* terminated." It reinforces that the decision is final and non-negotiable.

- Don't spend any time in the termination meeting trying to convince the individual that your actions are fair or right or appropriate. That person does not have to agree with you on the validity of the termination; they just need to understand the decision has been made.

- Don't apologize for terminating someone's employment. It is your job, and had the employee followed policies, the termination would not be happening. *You* did not do it—he or she did.

- Don't say things like, "This is really hard for me" or "I know how you're feeling." Again, this meeting is not about you. There's no need for you to try to connect with the individual you are letting go. Be respectful but quick and get it done.

- Jot a few sentences on a notepad about the conversation, especially if the individual mentioned something about her lawyer or the situation not being over. Note what was said and any behaviors that the individual exhibited during the meeting.

- If the individual has been reasonable during the meeting, do not humiliate him by escorting him from the facility unless you have good cause to suspect an incident might occur.

- Be kind and compassionate—put yourself in that person's shoes.

CHAPTER TEN:

WHERE TO GO FROM HERE

"To get through the hardest journey we need take only one step at a time, but we must keep stepping."

-Chinese Proverb

We have covered a lot of HR territory, from recruitment and hiring, to discipline and termination. You may feel pretty good that many of the suggestions provided in this book have been things that you are regularly practicing and they are working well for you. You may also be overwhelmed by everything there is to know and do and are probably lamenting over where to even begin to make important changes that impact your team.

Take heart! Remember that you do not need to do everything at once! Remember, too, that nothing worth achieving is ever easy—if it was, everyone would do it! So, if you want the payoff, you need to put in the work. Start with a true assessment of the situation within your facility, your department, or your shift, whichever applies to you. Get input from members of your team (might I recommend the grouchiest ones?) who may look at things from a different perspective than you. Once you have identified areas of need, develop a list of goals you would like to accomplish, and dream big.

Break each goal into manageable steps. For example, if your goal is Improve Morale on the Second Shift," start with the question, "What would it look like if second shift had better morale?" Answers might include

- employees smile more and greet one another in the halls,
- there's more laughter heard from the break rooms,
- employees are offering to assist one another when their work is complete, and
- employees compliment one another, instead of complaining about one another.

Now decide how to encourage each of these behaviors in employees, for example,

- walk through the facility at 4:00 p.m., and hand out Jolly Ranchers to the jolly employees who are smiling when you see them;
- tag smiling staff with smiley-face stickers when they clock in, and tell them their residents want to see them smiling more often;
- do hallway high-fives with staff (very few will leave you hanging if you approach with a smile);
- post goofy cartoons or silly nursing-related jokes in the break room, and offer a free meal ticket when people submit a good one;
- develop a program where employees can recognize each other for being super-supportive, and let them cash in recognition cards for a lottery ticket or a free soda from the soda machine;

- encourage employees during staff meetings to recognize their superstar co-workers for special ways they have been team players over the past few weeks;

- post a photo of an employee who was complimented by co-workers with a note about what he did or why he is special; or

- devote a section of your employee newsletter to celebrating your employee superstars, with the focus on teamwork-related achievements.

You will need to be patient, but also celebrate each small success. This type of change is aimed at the culture of an organization, and it will not happen overnight. Keep a log of each success, and review it often. It will be what keeps you motivated to continue toward your goal, especially when you are feeling defeated by the setbacks that are sure to happen.

I love the phrase "have an attitude of gratitude." It is an excellent frame of mind for you as you begin to work toward making positive changes in your organization. One of the questions John Maxwell asks himself every day is, "How can I add value to another person today?" It is a question that you should ask yourself every day as a team leader. Adding value to one person at a time will lead to exponential growth in your respect and credibility with your team. Never forget that your most valuable resources in health care are your *human* resources.

Another way to almost instantly improve your credibility is to become an excellent manager of time—yours and everyone else's. This includes starting and ending meetings on time, keeping regular meetings and trainings consistent, and not interrupting others' work with your own issues that can wait for a more opportune time for the other person. All of these things show employees that you are a person of your word, that you appreciate and value their time, and that you know what they bring to the team is just as important as what you do.

While there are many areas where you can affect a change on your own, it will be imperative to have buy-in from people at the top of the chain of command if changes are to be accepted and encouraged. Make sure your supervisors, administrators, and the other decision-makers within your organization understand your goals, as well as what support might be needed from them to be successful. If financial support is needed, for example, for buying a box of candy bars or five lottery tickets each month, make sure you outline the benefits of the program when you explain its costs. Show that you have thought your plan through by having a system to evaluate the program's effectiveness, as well; then provide regular updates on the program to supervisors and make adjustments, as needed.

As with all new things, there will be those who think that any change is bad and that your ideas won't work here. I advise you to hear their words, but do not accept their negativity. Use their opposition to help you avoid mistakes or take into account potential problems, but do not let them discourage your enthusiasm, even if you fail. Learn to readjust your thinking to see failures as opportunities. As Thomas Edison said when he was attempting to create the first light bulb, "I have not failed. I've just found ten thousand ways that won't work."

Finally, utilize the wisdom of those who have come before you and done exceptional things. Reading the works of ZigZiglar, Norman Vincent Peale, Dale Carnegie, Napoleon Hill, Steven Covey, and John Maxwell can inspire you to achieve your goals, to believe in yourself, and to focus on what is important. Reading their books is like doing data entry on a computer: Putting positive, encouraging thoughts and ideas into your head helps you become more positive and encouraging in your life. Putting nothing in—or worse, putting in the negativity of disgruntled employees and defeated leaders—makes you feel more negative, disgruntled, and defeated yourself.

It is my sincere hope that in your reading you have found some ways to become a better leader in your long-term care community, and you are now prepared to set the course to move your team forward toward excellence. As you develop ways to improve relationships and hone your HR skills, I challenge you to remember this important thought from ZigZiglar,

"You don't have to be great to start, but you have to start to be great."

About the Author

Lori L. Dierolf grew up in Minersville, a small coal-mining town in Schuylkill County, Pennsylvania. She moved to Lancaster County in 1987 to attend Millersville University of Pennsylvania, where she earned her Bachelor's degree in psychology in 1991.

Lori began working in the long-term care industry as an HR professional in 1997 and in 2016 became owner of Open Door Training & Development, a company that provides engaging and enthusiastic educational opportunities for individuals who wish to develop their HR and leadership skills.

Having been touched by the lives of many special residents during her years in the retirement community industry, Lori is very passionate about supporting those whose lives have been impacted by the effects of dementia and Alzheimer's disease. She offers individual and group educational sessions for those caring for loved ones, as well as more formal training and speaking engagements for professional caregivers and other community organizations.

Lori has been married to her husband Jim since 2005 and has two children, Amber and Jackson. They live in Millersville, Pennsylvania.